Reading Power

Teaching Students to Think While They Read

Adrienne Gear

Pembroke Publishers Limited

DEDICATION

In memory of my dad, William Irvine Gear, who instilled in me a passion for literature and dedication to teaching, both of which have become an invaluable part of "my story."

© **2006 Pembroke Publishers**
538 Hood Road
Markham, Ontario, Canada L3R 3K9
www.pembrokepublishers.com

Distributed in the U.S. by Stenhouse Publishers
480 Congress Street
Portland, ME 04101-3400
www.stenhouse.com

We acknowledge the financial support of the Government of Canada through the Book Publishing Industry Development Program (BPIDP) for our publishing activities.

We acknowledge the assistance of the OMDC Book Fund, an initiative of the Ontario Media Development Corporation.

Library and Archives Canada Cataloguing in Publication

Gear, Adrienne
    Reading power : teaching students to think while they read / Adrienne Gear.

Includes index.
ISBN 13: 978-1-55138-203-6
ISBN 10: 1-55138-203-2
    1. Reading comprehension. 2. Reading (Elementary). I. Title.

LB1525.7.G42 2006   372.47   C2006-902667-X

Editor: Kat Mototsune
Cover design: John Zehethofer
Typesetting: Jay Tee Graphics

Printed and bound in Canada
9 8 7 6 5 4 3

Contents

Foreword

Reading Power is a reading comprehension program currently being implemented in many schools in Vancouver and across BC's lower mainland. It is a way of teaching reading comprehension that focuses readers' attention on their thinking as they read.

The Reading Power program was launched at Laura Secord Elementary School in Vancouver in October 2002. Initially it was developed for primary teachers at that school as an initiative towards their involvement in the Vancouver School Board's Early Literacy Project. From the moment at an Early Literacy meeting that I held up a napkin with a scrawled picture of a child with puzzle pieces over his head, the teachers of Laura Secord enthusiastically supported me and the idea of trying something different to help our students become better readers. In the years since then, they have unquestionably and willingly embraced Reading Power as the focus of their Early Literacy Project. They allowed me into their classrooms to participate and to witness the program as it evolved. They provided me with invaluable insights and suggestions as to how it could be improved, and were always eager to suggest their own favorite book title or to share their handouts, lessons, and extensions.

I have heard expressed during literacy conferences and symposiums that the greatest contribution to a child's literacy progress is exemplary teaching practices. I can say, without a doubt, that there is not one teacher at Laura Secord I had the privilege of teaching with who does not demonstrate exemplary teaching. This book would not have been possible without them. My thanks go to Amy Wou, Madeline Silva, Tina Gill, Deborah Hay, Tammi Sinniah, Vicky Liakouras, Julie Luciani, Faye MacLeod, Sarine Sran, Lauren Smith, Jodi McKay, Krista Forbes, Lesley Chambers, Nancy Hawkins, Viviana Verhage, Farzana Kassam, Dick Griffin, Kathy Green, Todd Millway, Jim Stevens, Phil Green, Sarah Gray, Sharon Kent, Zoi Brown, Hilary Uren, Sheri Duckles, Deborah Robinson, Berni Batchelor, Bernice Robinson, Mary Rickson, and Mike Goshko. My thanks also to the administrators who supported the implementation of Reading Power throughout the school: Kimberley Toye, Stephanie Sellars, Anna-Maria Niccoli-Mullet, and Kerri Wallen.

Acknowledgments

The expression "It takes a village" describes my sentiments when considering the number of people who, directly or indirectly, have been involved in *Reading Power*. This work is a reflection of many dedicated teachers, teacher-librarians, administrators, consultants, colleagues, friends, and family who have been supporting my efforts for many years. While it may not be possible to name them all, I will do my best to try.

I am especially grateful to Amy Wou, my colleague and friend, for her continued support and encouragement (over many cups of creamy Earl Grey), for her practical suggestions in the initial stages of developing Reading Power, and for helping me turn my vision into something that could be realistically implemented in a classroom. Thank you to Madeline Silva, Sarine Sran, Deborah Hay, and Amy Wou for their valuable insights, suggestions, and lesson contributions during the beginning stages. Special thanks to Tina Gill and her kindergarten class for teaching me the "Reading Power Theme Song."

I wish to thank the extraordinary students of Laura Secord Elementary School and many other Vancouver schools with whom I have worked and from whom I have learned so much. Their enthusiasm for Reading Power and their willingness to rise to the challenge of thinking about reading in a new way has made this journey enormously worthwhile. They have taught me more than I could ever teach them.

Special thanks go to the following teachers who contributed student samples and/or reproducibles for this book: Amy Wou, Madeline Silva, Tammi Sinniah, Viviana Verhage, Deborah Hay, Sarine Sran, Kathy Green, Carla Friesen, Kimberly Matterson, Brenda Boylan, Judy Reitenbach, Lorraine Bayne, Linda Kearns, Mary Anne Yu, Bernice Jay, Janine Reid, Rose Lemaire, Carrie Gelson, Anna Feddema, Gina Wong, Lisa Hoo, Wanda Salewski, Maria Maragos, Cheryl Burian, and John Dyer. I am grateful to them, not only for the samples, but for their continued effort to implement these lessons by adding, changing, creating, enhancing, and making them their own.

I continue to be inspired by the hundreds of teachers, teacher-librarians, and administrators with whom I have worked in the Vancouver School district during the past years. It is a privilege to be in a position where I am in contact with so many dedicated teachers in pursuit of enhancing their reading programs, not by a "quick fix" but by a deeper understanding of reading and thinking. Although it is not possible to mention them all, I would like to acknowledge some who have worked so hard to support the implementation of Reading Power in their schools by organizing workshops, Book Bins, and demo lessons, and by providing time for teachers to meet, reflect, and plan: Mary McConville (Henderson); Judy Fung (Edith Cavell); Donna Boardman (Mackenzie); Maria Maragos and Joanne Dale (Carleton); Andy-Powell Williams, Connie Robson, and Erin Gibbs (Brock); Nancy Cleveland and Celina Mau (Emily Carr); Carole Anne Veregin and Rosemary Thomas (Thunderbird); Judy Reitenbach and Lorraine Bayne (Selkirk); Nicky Mey (Champlain Heights); Anna Feddema (Weir); Madelaine Donatiello (Oppenheimer); Joan Storland and Sarah Gray (Kitchener); Kimberly Matterson (Nelson); Wendy Cameron (Wolfe); Barb Parrott (Selkirk Annex); Yvette Cassidy (Van Horne); Margaret Jorgensen (Seymour); Joanna Wood (Southlands); Roxanne Madryga (Cunningham); Mary Anne Yu and Bernice Jay (Olser); Catherine Feniak (Queen Alexander); Kathryn Buchan (Douglas); Georgina Arntzen (McQuinna); Delma Campbell (Norquay); Betty Iaquinta (Elsie Roy); Jacquie Hall (David Lloyd George); Betty Less (McBride Annex); Jeanette Mumford and Philip Moses (Sexsmith); Rosa Audia Maag and Patty Neibel (Nootka); Surinder Deo and Suzanne Morgan (Tecumseh); Mary Anne Grover and Natalie Moresette (Jules Quesnel); Dee Mochrie (Graham Bruce); Joanne Lloyd (Queen Elizabeth Annex); Denise North (Britannia); Ciara Corcoran and Tracey Macleod (West Point Grey Academy). I wish to extend a very special and sincere thank-you to Jim Harcott, teacher at Lord Kitchener Elementary, for demonstrating not only a desire to change his teaching practice but the courage to do so.

It is one thing to attend a workshop, but it is another to take ideas from a workshop and begin to implement them into classroom practice. Thank-you to the many teachers, teacher-librarians, administrators, and support teachers in the Richmond School district who have been instrumental in promoting Reading Power in their schools, in particular, Cheryl Burian, Laura Birarda, Carole Wilson, Ted Lim, May Oshiro, Sandy Haras and Jean-Ann Stene (thank you for the Smarties!), Adam Heeney, Don Dixon, Carol-Lyn Sakata, Darlene Shandola, Christy Domonokos, Susan Shackles, Nancy Kisbee, Nichole Kusch, Jane MacMillan, Sarah Loat, Leslie Sobotin, Gillian Partridge, Christel Brautigam, Dianne Tijman, Susan Tse, Jean Adshead, Gina Rae, Janice Novakowski, and Kathryn D'Angelo. In North Vancouver, my thanks to Kathy Fairbanks and the staff at Brooksbank Elementary School. In Maple Ridge, my sincere thanks to Delee Labelle; in Abbotsford, to Kim Kass, Carol Johnston, and Rob Carmichael; in Coquitlam, to Maureen Dockendorf, Joyce Jackman, Kelly Owens, Paulette Flood, and Kyme Wegrich, and a special thanks to Gloria Gustafson whose enthusiasm for Reading Power matches my own. Thanks to the wonderful teachers and consultants in Kamloops, in particular Judy Dunn, Kathie Peters, and Andrea Wallin, for their enormous support and enthusiasm for *Reading Power* and for making me feel so welcome when I visit. Special thanks to my dear friend Katie McCormack-Adams, amazing Kamloops teacher and extraordinary mother, for sharing her story of her son Jacob's "visualizing" and for sitting in the front row looking so proud. Thank-you to the wonderful teachers in Penticton for laughing at all my jokes, even the ones I did not intend to make, and special thanks to my new friend, Judy Scott, and my almost sister-in-law Heather Rose. I am grateful for the "twists" of Jennifer Gardner, Deanna Michaud, and Lynda Henney in Vernon. On the Sunshine Coast, my thanks to Fran Gamache, Bev Craig, and Gaetane Huska; and in the Queen Charlottes, to Jenny White and my sister, Alison Gear.

I'd like to acknowledge the incredible staff at Vancouver Kidsbooks, particularly owner Phyllis Simon, for providing an invaluable source for teachers and teacher-librarians of outstanding children's literature to support their literacy programs. The Kidsbooks staff have been instrumental in helping teachers from all over the province begin to create their Reading Power Book Bins, and I am grateful for all their help. Special thanks to Celeste Hamel and Joe Lopes, whose small discount bookstore in Kelowna, Celeste Books, has done big things to help teachers in the interior of BC purchase Reading Power books.

There are many people who have, over the years, inspired me to evolve into not only a teacher of students but a teacher of teachers. I am grateful to Ruth Wrinch, Vancouver administrator, who was my first mentor. She taught me, through example, the art of listening, and was instrumental in my pursuit of knowledge, change, and best classroom practice.

Jan Wells—teacher, author, and former Literacy Consultant in the Vancouver School Board—has been an enormous inspiration to me over the years. I am grateful for her continued support and encouragement throughout my teaching career, and for inviting me to share Reading Power with schools in the district. She has taught me, through example, to be a leader and learner, and to look for places to plant the seeds.

My sincere thanks to Stephanie Sellars, former vice-principal of Laura Secord, for her enormous support and invaluable input, and for enabling me to implement the Reading Power Program throughout the school.

To Gwen Bartnik, former Literacy Consultant for the Vancouver School Board—thank you for encouraging me to become a Literacy Mentor and for insisting that I join her and Mary Macchiusi for lunch. Thanks, also, to the other Literacy Mentors and consultants at the VSB with whom I have the privilege of working: Meredyth Kezar, Kimberly Matterson, Joan Storlund, Dianna Mezzarobba, Carla Friesen, Jodi Carson, Barb Mcbride, Brenda Boylan, Natalie Morissette, Sallie Boschung, Malena Oliveri, Marzena Michalowska, Shelagh Maguire, and Pat Parungao. Your dedication to your craft and your pursuit of excellence in the field of literacy continues to inspire me. Special thanks to Fabienne Goulet, French Immersion Mentor, for sharing her inspiring story about her son with me.

I wish to acknowledge and thank Pat Dymond, who has worked tirelessly with me over many months typing out the small handout that has turned into a rather large book! Thank you, Pat, for your patience and flexibility, and all the help you have given me.

Thanks to Mary Macchiusi at Pembroke, for believing that I did have a story to tell, for encouraging me to add "flesh" to content, and for saying "yes" twice; to Kat, my editor, for her patience in the process and for her invaluable help in organizing the structure of this book and for her clarity in the process.

To Cheryl, Anna, Laura, Jarma, Maria, Bonnie, Heather, and Stella—my wonderful book club friends—thank you for being my "highlight" once a month, for providing me a place to put theory into practice and for tolerating my adoration of each selection for almost four years. Engaging in rich, meaningful discussions about great books—I can't think of a better way to spend a Friday night, or anyone else I'd rather be spending it with.

Special thanks to my dearest friend, Cheryl Burian, teacher at Homma Tomakichi Elementary School in Richmond and founder of our book club, for her support of me and of Reading Power as it evolved from its earliest stages on a napkin until now. Thank you for inspiring me to pursue my passion, regardless of the disappointments and challenges that I faced along the way. You have always expected nothing less than the best from me, yet shown me nothing but love while I try to achieve it. I couldn't ask for a better friend.

Finally, to my family: my love and thanks to my mum, Sheila Gear, and my two sisters Alison and Janet, for their unwavering support and wisdom. I am eternally grateful to my husband, Richard Gatzke, who said to me once, "It must be very tiring living inside your head." He continues to keep me grounded in the important things and supports my numerous pursuits with quiet loyalty and love. Finally, I want to thank my two boys, Spencer and Oliver, who have, without *question, connected* me to the beauty and energy of the inquiring mind, and have *transformed* my *vision* of love.

Introduction

Influenced by the book *Strategies That Work: Teaching Comprehension to Enhance Understanding* by Stephanie Harvey and Anne Goudvis (2000), and by the work of many researchers in the field of reading comprehension, including David Pearson, the Reading Power program is designed to teach specific strategies to use during the reading process that enable students to engage in a more interactive, thoughtful reading experience and to improve comprehension. Central to the program is authentic children's literature for modeling demonstrations, practice, and independent reading.

Comprehension Research

In the 1970s, an educator and researcher by the name of David Pearson, at the time a professor at the University of Michigan, embarked on a study of proficient readers. In lay terms, he wanted to know what made "this child" a better reader than all "these other children." What was it that a reader, exceeding expectations for his or her grade level, was doing that enabled him or her to master both the code and the meaning of the text? During this extensive study, his team of researchers studied hundreds of proficient readers and, after many years and an enormous amount of data, determined several common strategies used by proficient readers that enabled them to make sense of the text. A condensed version of this research is what I describe as the "profile" of a proficient reader.

Profile of a Proficient Reader

A good reader is **metacognitive**—aware of and able to use and articulate the following strategies in order to interact with the text and enhance meaning.

1. **Make Connections.** A good reader is able to draw from background knowledge and personal experiences while reading to help create meaning from the text.

2. **Ask Questions.** A good reader asks both literal and inferential questions before, during, and after reading to clarify meaning and deepen understanding.

3. **Visualize.** A good reader is able to create multi-sensory images in the "mind's eye" while reading to help make sense of the text.

4. **Determine Importance.** A good reader is able to sort through information in the text, select key ideas, and remember them.

5. **Draw Inferences.** A good reader knows that not all information is included in a text, and is able to reasonably "fill in," hypothesize, and predict, based on evidence in the text.

6. **Analyze and Synthesize.** A good reader is able to break down information and to draw conclusions based on both the text and his or her own thinking.

7. **Monitor Comprehension.** A good reader is aware when understanding is being compromised and is able to stop, go back, and reread in order for understanding to occur.

Thirty years later, David Pearson's research is now finding its way into teacher education, professional development, and classroom practice. The common strategies used by proficient readers are now being taught to readers of all grades and all levels of reading. Simply stated, if these strategies are what research has found to what good readers do to understand text, then this is what we need to be teaching our not-so-good-readers to do.

I had the pleasure of hearing David Pearson speak at a conference in Vancouver. I sat in the front row, clapping very loudly. (During his presentation, I wished I had a lighter with me—as at a rock concert—to shine and wave in support of his wise words.) He spoke of his research, and of implementing change in the way we need to think and teach students to read. Reading, he stated, is not simply mastering the code. Reading is both the code and meaning behind that code: teaching reading is both teaching the code and teaching students how to make the text meaningful for them. And, while many teachers make the assumption that once the code is mastered, so too is comprehension, we are now realizing that if we want our students to acquire the ability to comprehend texts, we need to balance our reading instruction to include explicit teaching both in decoding and in comprehension. The work of Stephanie Harvey and Anne Goudvis, and of Debbie Miller, much of which is based on David Pearson's research, reflects the complexity of comprehension and its being a separate, yet equally important, aspect of reading. They state, "Reading demands a two-pronged attack. It involves cracking the alphabetic code to determine the words and thinking about those words to construct meaning" (Harvey & Goudvis, 2000, p. 5).

How these strategies help readers develop a deeper and more meaningful understanding of text is becoming evident in many classrooms across the province. The new British Columbia Language Arts Integrated Resource Package (IRP) outlines many of these strategies within the context of reading instruction.

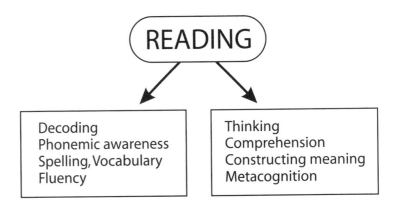

This graphic helps illustrate the point made by Harvey and Goudvis. The skills listed on the left are those skills essential to mastering the code, and are generally taught in the early primary grades. They are the basics of beginning reading instruction—taught in a variety of different approaches and methods, but certainly the main focus in the early primary Language Arts programs. Often the assumption is made that, once students have mastered the code (made up of the skills listed on the right), comprehension occurs naturally. But this is true for very few students. David Pearson's research points to comprehension as a separate aspect of reading, one that requires the same amount of direct instruction and teaching time as the decoding skills. "Once thought of as a natural result of decoding plus oral language, comprehension is now viewed as a much more complex process involving knowledge, experience, thinking and teaching" (Fielding & Pearson, pp. 62–67).

In other words, if we are to help improve our students' ability to comprehend text and learn to actively construct meaning for themselves, we need to devote as much direct instructional time teaching *thinking* as we do teaching *decoding*. Considering the number of instructional minutes primary teachers spend on teaching code, that would mean significant changes in the reading programs of many teachers. Reading instruction can no longer be considered the responsibility of early primary teachers; it is the responsibility of all teachers. All teachers need to consider themselves teachers of reading, and reading instruction must continue throughout all elementary and high-school grades. If mastering the code is only one aspect of learning to read, then teaching the code is only one aspect of reading instruction. Children need to learn that reading is not simply words on a page, but what those words mean to them. Teaching how to make sense of those words is just as important as teaching how to read them.

How the Reading Power Program Began

"There are literally hundreds of strategies we can choose to teach our students how to become better readers. The key is, everyone on your staff chooses the same ones."
—David Pearson, from a speech at Vancouver Technical Secondary, Fall 2003

Several years ago, the Vancouver School Board initiated a program called the Early Literacy Project. Its aim was to support teachers and students in their goal to improve literacy in the primary grades, and it has since evolved into the Later Literacy Project that supports intermediate teachers and students. Schools involved in the project participate in professional development in early literacy, hold monthly project meetings, are given training in reading assessment and running records, and are provided with funds for classroom visits and meetings with literacy mentors, as well as funds to increase their supply of appropriate reading material for all reading levels.

In 2001, the school where I was teaching, Laura Secord Elementary, joined the Early Literacy Project. During the first year in the project, one of our goals was to choose a literacy focus for our school. After several meetings, it was decided that we would spend our first few years in the project focusing on reading, more specifically on comprehension. We had spent the previous few years focusing on phonemic awareness, but had concerns that our students were not understanding much of what they were now able to decode. My question, when a Grade 2 student proudly tells me that he just finished "reading" a Harry Potter book, is "Did you actually *read* Harry Potter, or did you *de-code* it?" It was during those early meetings and discussions on the literacy goals of our school that my thoughts turned to Stephanie Harvey and Anne Goudvis' book, *Strategies That Work*. I reviewed the book and pulled out things that I thought could be implemented easily, adding my own ideas and my passion for children's literature. Reading Power was born.

Simplicity was my priority in developing this program. I knew how hard teachers work and how many demands are placed on us each year, so I knew that adding one more thing to the teaching plate was not going to be something everyone

When streamlining the Profile of a Proficient Reader, I changed "synthesize" to "transform" because I felt it was simpler language for young children. Most children are familiar with a "transformer" toy that changes from one form to another. The notion of a change in thinking seemed to be to be easier to describe to a young child by using the word "transform."

"Through language, your students learn how to become strategic thinkers, not merely strategy users."
—Peter Johnston, *Choice Words*

would welcome. I also knew that we, as a staff, had already been implementing many strategies from many different sources.

If I passed out the Profile of a Proficient Reader (pages 9–10) to my colleagues and said, "These are the strategies we need to be teaching our kids to help them become better readers," it would likely be filed, and "reading" would have carried on in classrooms as before. I knew that in order for us to try something new in the classroom, it needed to be simple and practical. I looked carefully over the profile of proficient readers and decided that seven strategies were simply too many to realistically expect primary teachers to teach and apply to their reading program, so I chose five of them: connect, question, visualize, infer, and synthesize. The strategies I did not choose are in no way less important. These five were chosen simply because of a belief that they were the ones that students could best learn and that teachers could most easily implement.

The strategies you choose—whether they be from the list of strategies that make up the Profile of a Proficient Reader, from the reading powers, or from another source—and the number you choose to introduce during the course of a year are not important. What is important is that everyone on your staff makes a commitment to intentionally integrate the strategies and the "language of thinking" into their daily practice. I have found that, in many schools, these same strategies are being taught, but teachers are using slightly different language to teach them. Creating a common language across the grades in a school becomes instrumental in a child's development as a reader. Common language, weaving through the fabric of the classrooms in a school, creates a quilt of understanding.

One caution is worth noting here. I have heard, on more than one occasion, teachers who have attended workshops and are successfully integrating Reading Power into their classrooms say, "Oh, I don't need to do guided reading [whole-class instruction, phonics, world walls, literacy centres, writers workshop, buddy reading, or other components of a balanced literacy program] because I'm doing Reading Power." Reading Power is *one* component of a balanced literacy program, but it should never be considered the *only* component. I like to think of Reading Power as an additional "layer" to your reading instruction; it should not be—nor do I promote it as—a separate and isolated entity. Certainly there are many ways that Reading Power might spill over into other areas, but a balanced literacy program should reflect a variety of instructional methods, content, and practices.

1 What is Reading Power?

For me, an activity is the thing you do, while a strategy is the way in which you do it.

The five reading strategies in the Reading Power program are called reading "powers," because the word "strategy" has been used to describe just about anything done in the classroom, and is often used interchangeably with the word "activity." The five reading powers are, in fact, reading strategies.

Reading Power
- is based on research that looks at strategies used by proficient readers.
- teaches students that reading is thinking.
- teaches students to be metacognitive, or aware of their thinking.
- creates a "language of thinking" in your classroom.
- teaches students five powers to enhance their understanding of the fiction texts they are reading: the powers to Connect, Question, Visualize, Infer, and Transform.
- encourages students to have "busy brains" while they read.
- provides a concrete visual tool to help teach the five reading powers.
- exposes students to a wide range of rich, engaging literature —including both old classics and wonderful new titles.
- helps build a common language of reading comprehension throughout your classroom and your school.
- can be used to enhance your writing program.
- is respectful of children's thinking and encourages them to think beyond the pages of the books they are reading.
- celebrates the students' voices in the classroom and allows for their thinking, their connections, their images, and their ideas to make a difference.
- will change the way you and your students read and think.

Reading, Thinking, and Teaching

A mother and son, who is not yet school age, sit facing each other on the floor in the living room, each reading a book. Their "noisy reading" time, when Mom reads aloud to her child, is over, and now they are sharing in their "quiet reading" ritual. Mom senses her son is not engaged on this particular day, and notices that he keeps looking up from his book to stare at her. After a while, she asks him what he is doing.

"I'm watching to see what happens."

"What happens in my book?" she asks.

"No… what happens when you read."

"Oh," she answers, and goes back to reading.

The boy continues to watch his mother intently while she reads. "Mom ," the boy asks finally, "what really happens to you when you read?"

This young boy has, in his simplicity, asked a most profound question. The notion of "something happening" while we read is the essence of comprehension. The "something happening" is the interactive construction of meaning inside our heads, which creates understanding. The "something happening" can be difficult to see, difficult to understand, difficult to assess, and difficult to teach. And sadly, the "something happening" does not naturally occur inside all readers.

Because comprehension is not tangible and can be subjective, it is a subject that many teachers do not necessarily delve into the first week in their school year. Certainly it was not, up until a few years ago, a subject that found a spot on my weekly timetable or a place in my "shape of the day." In fact, there was no time in my school year that I could honestly say was devoted to direct comprehension instruction. Why? If I look back on my own education, I do not recall any reading instruction other than the decoding and phonemic awareness I received in the early primary grades. In university, I do not recall any methodology courses on comprehension instruction.

I began my teaching career as an intermediate teacher. As a new intermediate teacher, I considered my job to be somehow more interesting than that of my primary teacher colleagues. Thanks to the hard work of those primary teachers, my students could, for the most part, already read when they came into my class in September. I'm embarrassed to admit that I clearly remember saying to a friend that the reason I enjoyed teaching intermediate grades so much was that I didn't have to teach reading and could do "the fun stuff" with the students. I truly believed the expression, "Learn to read in the primary grades and read to learn in the intermediate grades." I never considered myself a "teacher of reading." We "did" reading in my class, but it was not something that I "taught." I did not need to teach reading—my students already knew how.

I now realize that my rendition of "doing reading" was, "Read this chapter and then answer these questions"—what is now termed "assign and assess" teaching. And when a student was able to answer only two out of the ten questions correctly, what was I doing to help? Usually I handed back the notebook with the message, "*Please do your corrections,*" along with a sparkly sticker stating, "Good effort!" or "Nice printing!" The thought of it now makes me cringe—how little I was doing to help my students become better readers. Sure, my students were read to every day; my classroom was overflowing with literature; we did novel studies, book reports, story maps, letters to the authors, book talks; we wrote reading response logs, made dioramas, created posters, did readers theatre, and did all the "fun stuff" that I believed fell under the category of teaching reading.

Looking back, I wonder how many of those activities represented a deep understanding of text. Certainly my students enjoyed the process and were proud of their products. But I realize now that I was not, under any circumstances, teaching them how to use their experiences and their knowledge to make sense of what they were reading. I was at the helm of a sinking ship, handing out brushes and paint to my students and teaching them how to paint the decks. Showing children that reading is not just words on a page, helping them see what of ourselves we bring to those words, is perhaps the single most important thing we can do, not only to keep our ships afloat, but to send them full-speed ahead.

Current Reading Practice

When my school joined the Vancouver School District's Early Literacy Project, I remember thinking about my current classroom practices. I came from a school of very dedicated teachers who were all working towards enhancing their classroom practice in the area of literacy. Many, including myself, had attended after-school workshops and professional development on balanced literacy, and had already begun implementing many of these strategies. When trying to implement change, I believe it is important to begin to look at the things one is already doing well, so I remember a meeting where my colleagues and I discussed and brainstormed all the literacy initiatives, strategies, and activities we were currently practising in our classrooms. The list was long and represented a wealth of good classroom practices. After analyzing this list carefully, I found it interesting to see exactly where our reading instruction occurred in the reading process.

Three Stages of Teaching Reading

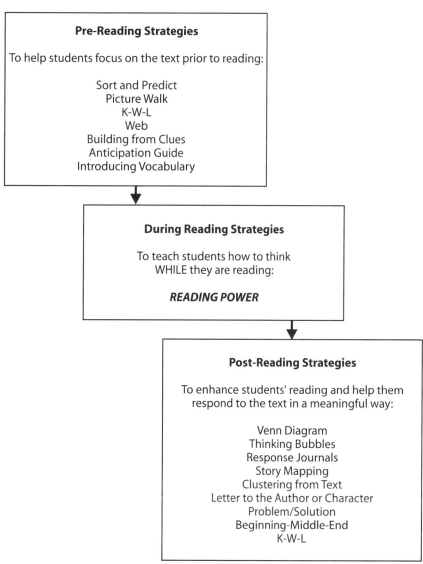

Pre-Reading Strategies

To help students focus on the text prior to reading:

Sort and Predict
Picture Walk
K-W-L
Web
Building from Clues
Anticipation Guide
Introducing Vocabulary

During Reading Strategies

To teach students how to think
WHILE they are reading:

READING POWER

Post-Reading Strategies

To enhance students' reading and help them
respond to the text in a meaningful way:

Venn Diagram
Thinking Bubbles
Response Journals
Story Mapping
Clustering from Text
Letter to the Author or Character
Problem/Solution
Beginning-Middle-End
K-W-L

If we look at the reading process as three equally important stages—pre-reading, during-reading, and post-reading—everything we were doing in our reading program fell in either the pre- or the post- stage (see The Three Stages of Reading Instruction chart on page 15). Prior to reading, we spent time building up interest in the text with predictions, picture walks, and K–W–L. Then either the students would read independently or we would read to them. After reading, the students would be engaged in various post-reading activities.

There was a big gap in the during-reading stage of my teaching. In other words, what were we teaching our students to do when the book was in their hands and their eyes were on the words? And, according to Pearson's research, comprehension occurs while we are in the act of reading; therefore, those during-reading strategies hold the key to understanding. I realized that teaching children specific strategies for the during-reading process was the piece that had been missing from my reading program, and the hole left by that missing piece kept getting bigger each year. As a teacher, I consider myself first and foremost a learner. Having learned not only what was missing in my practice, but trying to find a way to fill in the missing piece, I was learning the most valuable lesson of my teaching journey.

Teaching the Reading Powers

In this model, the younger primary students do not learn the last two strategies of Inferring and Transforming. But don't underestimate the power of Kindergarten and early primary students to learn the strategies. If you integrate the language into your classroom and model with the right books, I believe that even very young children can learn these higher-level thinking skills.

The five reading powers do not need to be introduced or taught in any particular order, as they are not dependent on each other. In terms of a hierarchy of skills, however, Inferring and Transforming are definitely more complex, and I recommend not starting with these. Connecting and Visualizing tend to be easier for the younger students to grasp and are able to be learned and practised by students who are not yet reading independently.

The first year of implementation might look like this:

Kindergarten: Connect, Visualize (March)
Grade 1:   Connect, Visualize, Question (January)
Grade 2:   Connect, Question, Visualize, Infer (November)
Grade 3:   Connect, Question, Visualize, Infer, Transform (September)

Using *Reading Power*

Now that the theory and background behind Reading Power is clear, we can focus on the practical application, the "how to" of explicit teaching of comprehension. There are three important components of the Reading Power program:

1. The **Reading Powers Model** (see page 20) represents the metacognitive piece of Reading Power and the importance of providing your students with the "big picture" of what reading and thinking are.
2. The **Book Bins** are a way to organize the literature you will use, and reinforce the importance of selecting appropriate books to use in modeling, teaching, and practising the strategies.
3. The **Method of Instruction** is most important: how to actually teach these strategies in your classroom.

Chapters 3 to 7 will take you deeper into each of the Reading Power strategies. Each of these chapters begins with a song or chant to use as a teaching tool, some insight into the strategy, and suggestions on how to introduce the concept to your students. Then a series of teacher-directed and independent lessons follow, taking you through the steps of modeling, guiding, and independent practice, and including suggested book titles for each lesson. You will find student samples and reproducible charts and templates, and also an extensive list of suggested books for each Reading Power.

Metacognition

"Metacognition" was a new buzz word when I was doing courses for my Masters degree at the University of British Columbia. Although I did not understand it fully, I certainly made the effort to insert it into my papers as often as I could, so I could present myself to my learned professors as being in touch with the current lingo. Now, many years and experiences later, the concept of *metacognition* or "awareness of thinking" has become paramount in my teaching practice. I want students not only to think while they read, but to be aware that thinking is a prerequisite for becoming a successful reader.

> Good readers are metacognitive. That means they have an awareness, or an understanding, that their brain needs to be doing specific things while they're reading to help them understand the text better.

Several years ago, I had a classroom experience in my classroom that was instrumental to my teaching and learning. I was teaching a Grade 5 class and, during silent reading, would call students up to my desk individually to read aloud to me. I made notes about their miscues, reading strategies, and fluency, and then usually asked them a few questions about the text. This day, it was Simon's turn to come to my desk. Simon was an ESL learner, having immigrated to Canada with his family from Guatemala when he was three. He was a lively, personable child who communicated well. He happily came to my desk, sat beside me, and began reading aloud from his chapter book. He read with fluency and expression, and demonstrated many of the decoding strategies he had learned in his previous grades. I was impressed with his reading and told him so. Had I stopped there, I would have made some huge assumptions of what kind of reader he was. But then I began asking him a few questions from the story. Simon was not able to answer a single question. I remember feeling completely shocked at his lack of understanding, and wondered how it could be possible for a student to be reading the words from a text so well, yet not have a single idea about what he was reading. I remember turning to Simon and asking him, "Aren't you thinking about the story when you read it?" After a moment's pause, Simon turned to me and said, "What does thinking look like?" It was probably the most important question anyone has ever asked me. At the time, I could not really answer him: "Thinking is… well… it's just thinking!" was certainly not the answer he was looking for. Now I wish that I could find Simon and tell him that I can finally answer his question.

> "Excellent reading! Well done. Now, I'm just going to ask you a few questions about what you just read…"

Simon's profound question has stayed with me over the years. I think many teachers have had similar experiences with their own "Simon": children who become so focused on the code that they forget to really think about the story. Simon showed me a missing piece to the reading puzzle. I was doing so much with my students in terms of reading, yet the part I was *not* doing seemed to be the most important—"Whoops! Sorry, kids, I almost forgot to tell you this tidbit of information: when you read, you also need to think"!

> Good readers know that reading is not just being able to say the words on the page. Reading is being able to say the words and also to *think* about what those words mean to them.

Good readers know that in order to be successful readers, they need to be thinking about the story while they are reading.

It became important to me, when developing Reading Power for students, to let them in on the secret: The secret to becoming a successful reader is to learn to think while you read. And I wanted to show children the answer to Simon's question: *What does thinking look like?* Providing children with something concrete and visual so that they could really see what a "thinking brain" looks like when it's reading. It was essential that this metacognition be somehow incorporated into Reading Power as a concrete image that could be a point of reference. Simply put, if Simon's head was empty, I needed to fill it up with five reading powers. And that was how the Reading Powers Model (see page 20) was born. I roughly drew it on a napkin and presented it to my staff, then drew and colored one for every primary classroom in my school. The common language of reading comprehension naturally emerged from the use of the Reading Powers Model, and the Reading Power slogan became "Fill Your Head with Reading Power."

It is important to mention that, after teaching Reading Power to hundreds of children, it has become clear to me that children's brains are not empty at all. In fact, their brains are already filled with these strategies. The only problem is, they aren't necessarily aware of them. Our job, as teachers, is not to fill their brains, but to focus their brains on the cognitive strategies that are already in their heads, and to provide them with the language to describe them.

ENHANCING METACOGNITION

Good Readers…	We Can Help By…
• use specific strategies while they read to help make sense of the text	• providing students with a common language of strategies used by proficient readers
• are metacognitive, or aware that their thinking plays an important role in their understanding of the text	• introduce students to metacognition—an awareness of thinking
• pay attention to their "thinking voice" while they read to help them make sense of the text	• model think-alouds so that the students can begin to see what thinking looks and sounds like

2   The Components of the Reading Power Program

The Reading Powers Model

Helping Students Become Metacognitive

Young children know that, when they read, they need to be actively using their eyes and often their mouths. But how many of them are aware that their brains also need to be active? It was important that this metacognitive awareness be somehow incorporated into the teaching of Reading Power so that the students could have a concrete image of what needs to be going on inside their heads as they read.

The Reading Powers Model is an interactive, visual prompt for the during-reading process; see page 20. Each poster depicts a child's head and shoulders, and the phrase "Fill Your Brain with Reading Power!" at the top. There are five separate, removable puzzle pieces that fit together and can be superimposed on the child's head. Each piece is labeled with a different reading power. As each reading power is introduced and taught, the appropriate puzzle piece is placed inside the image of the child's head. The idea behind the puzzle is that the pieces fit together to create the ideal proficient reader—"A POWER-ful brain reads well."

Because proficient readers often move from one strategy to another within a single reading experience, it is important to teach these reading powers accumulatively rather than separately. New pieces are added as new reading powers are introduced, but the pieces are never removed once placed in the head.

Good readers have busy brains when they read.

Students will see that the brain becomes filled as their metacognitive knowledge of their thinking develops, demonstrating that good readers have many different things going on in their heads while they read.

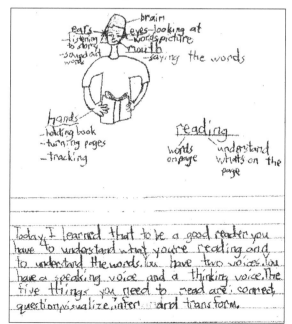

The Reading Powers Model

Name: _____   Date: _____

Fill Your Brain with Reading Power!

CONNECT

QUESTION   VISUALIZE   INFER

TRANSFORM

The Big Picture: Introducing the Thinking Brain

"When Howard reads, he has a busy brain."

I usually begin my first Reading Power lesson with this question: What parts of your body do you use when you read?" It is a good question to ask, and I have had some VERY interesting answers. Young children often answer "hands" first, with the thought of holding the book. Other answers quickly follow: hands, mouth, eyes, ears. But "the brain" is not an answer that is very often given. Why? I think that we, as teachers, probably do not often refer to the brain when we talk about reading, so it should not really surprise us that our students aren't aware of the brain as an active part of reading.

I then bring out the Reading Powers Model and explain to the students that Howard (each head should be given a name!) is a good reader. With the puzzle pieces in hand, I go over, in brief, each of the reading powers, to help the students to see the "big picture" more clearly:

Just like your eyes and hands have special jobs to do while you are reading, your brain has special jobs too.

The reason I know Howard is a good reader is that when Howard reads, his brain is busy. And if we could look inside Howard's head while he was reading, we would see five things going on in there. We call these five things "reading powers" because they've helped Howard become a powerful reader. Let's look inside Howard's brain to see what exactly is going on in there when he reads.

(I have very young children use their magical "X-ray glasses"
so they can look inside Howard's brain and watch while
the pieces are placed inside.)

If your Reading Powers Model and pieces have been laminated, use tape, velcro, or sticking gum on the back of each piece, so they can easily be placed and removed.

One thing that Howard does in his brain when he reads, to help him understand the story, is called *Connect*. That means that Howard might be reading about something that reminds him of something that happened to him once. Or he might be reading about a character that reminds him of himself or someone he knows. Or he might be reading a book that reminds him of another book he's read. And when that happens, it's called a *connection*.

(Place *Connect* piece in head.)

Another thing Howard does inside his head while he reads, to help him understand the story better, is to ask *Questions*. Sometimes teachers ask him questions after he's finished reading, but good readers ask questions *while* they read.

(Place *Question* piece in head.)

Now Howard is reading chapter books and novels, and most of these books do not have pictures in them. But Howard can read a story and, while he's reading, he can make the pictures right in his head. That is called *Visualizing*, and good readers visualize when they read. Visualizing is making pictures in your head.

(Place *Visualize* piece in head.)

Another thing that Howard can do while he reads is called *Inferring*. That might be a word that you have never heard before, but good readers infer while they read. Howard knows that not all authors write everything down in words. Some authors leave clues in their pictures and stories, and it's up to Howard to try to figure out what the author is trying to say. It's like he's filling in, in his head, what is not written on the page.

(Place *Infer* piece in head.)

The last thing that happens to Howard when he reads certain books is that he is actually *Transformed*. That doesn't mean he turns into a robot or a building, but it does mean that some changes happen inside his head. To transform is to change, and sometimes Howard's thinking changes while he's reading.

(Place *Transform* piece in head.)

(Hold an open book up to the Reading Powers Model.)

Let's watch Howard read for a while. Oh… Howard just made a connection. Now he's wondering something…. Now he's visualizing…. Now he's making another connection…. Now he's inferring…. Wow! Howard's brain is certainly busy, isn't it?

Well, that's what Howard's busy, thinking brain looks like while he's reading. Isn't that amazing?! Each of these reading powers helps him understand what he's reading. And because he's been reading this way for a long time, he's able to use the reading powers at the same time. He goes back and forth between them while he's reading—on one page he might ask a question, on the next page he might make a connection, then on another page he might make a picture in his head. But it's a little hard to do them all at once, so this year we are going to learn them one at a time. And I'll tell you something that might surprise you—you have all of these reading powers in your brains already, you just might not know it!

Children have often laughed at Howard, calling him Rainbow Brain and Helmet Head, but the Reading Powers Model has provided them with a concrete visual that they might not otherwise have. At my school, this visual has been the focal point for many children's conversations. One class may join another class for buddy reading and recognize the Model, but see a different piece inside the head. Different Brains have been given different names, and that becomes a conversation point as well.

Each time I begin a new reading power, I always go back to Howard and review the big picture with my students:

Why are we learning this again? We are learning this because good readers think while they read, and this thinking helps them understand the story better. Thinking looks different to every person because each of us has different ideas and experiences stored in our heads. But if we all learn to use our thinking brains by making connections or asking questions or making pictures in our heads, we will learn to how to understand the story better.

It is always exciting for me to hear of people who attend a Reading Power workshop and are inspired to take what they learn and adapt it to fit the needs of their classroom or school. Jennifer Garner, formerly Literacy Consultant in Vernon and currently a vice-principal in that district, is working on implementing many of the ideas and strategies from Reading Power throughout her school. She told me of a twist she has put on the Reading Powers Model. Students were involved in creating their own posters for each classroom, while Jennifer adapted the "brain pieces" for each grade level. For example, in Kindergarten, the students are learn-

After this first lesson introducing the Reading Powers Model, I often ask students to write a little reflection about what they learned.

ing Connect and Visualize, so those two puzzle pieces have been enlarged to fit into the head of the Kindergarten Model; in Grade 1, they are learning Connect, Visualize, and Question, so the Grade 1 Models have three pieces inside the head; and so on. She has also incorporated these strategies to include non-fiction, so her students are able to learn them simultaneously what Connecting looks like with a fiction text and what Connecting looks like with a non-fiction piece. I know of another teacher who had her class make self-portraits of their own heads. As she taught each new strategy, the students added a piece to their own mini-posters. When intermediate teachers have had their classes design their own Models, I've seen many unique hairstyles, clothes, and face piercings. How you develop or create this piece is up to you, but I do believe it is essential to somehow create a visual you can refer to: "This is what thinking looks like."

The Reading Power Theme Song

After the introduction lesson, the students of Tina Gill's Kindergarten class created the Reading Power Theme Song (below) and sang it for me, shouting the word "Brain" each time they sang it. Having five-year-olds sing a song about metacognition was most inspiring! I asked them why they were shouting the word "Brain" in the song, and one boy told me that it was "because the brain is so important when you read!" When I began teaching Reading Power to the intermediate students, I "borrowed" Mrs. Gill's Kindergarten class to sing the song to the bigger kids.

Mrs. Gill's class inspired me to create a song or chant to accompany each Reading Power. They can be taught as you introduce each new Reading Power and will help to reinforce the key ideas for each strategy. As my own class helped me write many of the verses, feel free to replace or add your own. I know of schools in Vancouver who are reinforcing the common language throughout the school through these songs, singing the songs at weekly school assemblies as the school focuses on each of the strategies.

Connect Song: page 34
Question Song: page 51
Visualize Chant and Song: page 65
Infer Song: page 81
Transform Chant: page 97

❊   ❊   ❊

Reading Power Theme Song
(to the tune of "Head & Shoulders")

Hands and mouth and
Eyes and BRAIN!
Eyes and BRAIN!
Eyes and BRAIN!
Hands and mouth and
Eyes and BRAIN!
High-five Reading Power!

❊   ❊   ❊

The Reading Power Book Bins

"For the price of a bowl of soup, I bought today at an old bookshop a volume infinitely valuable. All the way home on the train I read it; I was enlarged, I acquired merit, I added to my life."
—David Grayson

"Great books are central to teaching comprehension."
— Harvey & Goudvis, *Strategies That Work*

Picture books are not just for use in primary grades. In fact, many of the picture books available now I would consider too challenging, both in language and in theme, for younger readers.

Connect Booklist: page 42
Question Booklist: page 57
Visualize Booklist: page 73
Infer Booklist: page 90
Transform Booklist: page 106

On the first day of my Language Arts methodology course at the University of British Columbia many years ago, the professor, a woman by the name of Clare Staubs, entered the small room in the Ponderosa Building and began her lecture by reading aloud the first chapter of *The Great Gilly Hopkins* by Katherine Patterson. She told us, on that first day, that the single most important thing that we could do as teachers was to read aloud to our students every day. She began every lecture after that by reading another chapter from the book and, while some in her class may have been insulted by her read-alouds, I was forever changed. That experience had perhaps a more profound impact on me as a teacher than anything else I learned in any methodology course. I made a commitment to myself when I graduated that I was going to do just what Clare Staubs suggested. In my twenty years of teaching I have made many mistakes, but reading aloud to my class every day was something I did very well. No matter what the grade, no matter what was going on in the day, I have read aloud to my students every day they walked into my classroom. Reading aloud to students every day is my responsibility as a teacher, but for me it has also been a privilege. The literature that is available to children, teens, and young adults now is so extraordinarily rich, stunningly beautiful, and profound that we would be doing our students an enormous disservice if we did not share it with them. Books have "added to my life" and have certainly added to the lives of my students.

I encourage intermediate teachers to use picture books in their classrooms when introducing each of the strategies. David Pearson speaks about how he believes that, if teachers continue to try to teach students new reading strategies using texts that are "at the edge of their competence," students will have a much more difficult time grasping the new strategy and applying it to their reading; whereas if we bring the reading level down slightly to teach and practise the strategy, the students will have a far easier time learning and applying it. This supports my belief that by using picture books that are at a slightly less challenging reading level to teach a strategy, we can give our students a better chance of seeing, learning, and understanding the strategy. Intermediate children are thrilled to be given permission to read picture books, and enjoy the experience tremendously. I have had Grade 7 students fight over who gets *No, David!* books by David Shannon to practise Connecting, or leaping up to grab *The Cinder-Eyed Cats* for Visualizing.

Reading Power opens the door to literature for both teachers and students, and introduces them to an extraordinary range of titles, authors, and illustrators. Once I became familiar with the type of books that support each strategy, it became difficult to read a new book without thinking about which strategy I might use it for. During workshops, teachers often tell me of books they know that are not on the list that would be "perfect for Connecting" or "perfect for Visualizing." I encourage you to add your own favorites to the lists in this book. Certain books just lend themselves well to a certain strategy, and it is obvious what bin you would put them in. Other books tend to fit in more than one. I know when a book is good when I don't know what bin to put it in!

In as much as I am committed to read aloud every day, I must admit that at times there used to be no rhyme or reason for my daily read-alouds. I often just read a book to my students because I liked it, it suited the special occasion of the calendar year, or I had had a recent visit to a bookstore. But now, Reading Power has given me the structure under which all my read-alouds now fall. I specifically choose books that support the strategy I am teaching and intentionally integrate the language while I read. It is for this reason that I created the Book Bins. The Book Bins are not a necessity and, let's face it, can be an expensive endeavor, but they have made life a little easier for the teachers who use them. There is not enough time in a teacher's day, and having all the books in one place, ready to go, has certainly proved to be a huge time saver.

I love so many books, but some books just work better for teaching and practising a strategy than others. I decided to create Reading Power Book Bins that each contain a separate collection of books specifically selected because they lend themselves best to a particular strategy. Books are stored in a plastic tub to be signed out by teachers, and are rotated every four to six weeks.

Some schools select five or six books for each strategy that they keep in separate "Gem bags." These Gems are special books that the teacher uses for modeling lessons or guided practice, and are not included in the Book Bins with books students use for independent practice. In each Reading Power chapter, you will find two separate book lists: the first is for recommended Gems, books found to be particularly good for modeling lessons; it is followed by a list of books to choose from to create your Book Bins for the students.

The turnover of children's books is enormous and, as one title goes out of print, there are three more great new titles released. After conferring with several Teacher Librarians in the district, I have decided to keep some "out of print" books included on this list. Some of these out of print books are classics and there always seems to be copies of them hiding on library shelves, waiting to be read.

Here are lists of my Top Picks, favorite new books for both Primary and Intermediate grades for each of the five Reading Powers. More extensive lists are at the end of each strategy chapter.

After one or two years, some teachers have found it beneficial to purchase a few new Gems for each of the strategies. This way, the modeling lessons are fresh and interesting for the students. There are so many children's books being published each year, it isn't difficult to find a few great new titles to add to the collections.

Top Picks for Reading Power: Primary

CONNECT (FOR K–1)

Catherine & Laurence Anholt, *Good Days Bad Days*
Vicki Churchill, *Sometimes I Like to Curl Up in a Ball*
Paul Fleischmann, *Rondo in C*
Sam McBratney, *I'm Sorry*
Colin McNaughton, *Once Upon An Ordinary School Day*
David McPhail, *Sisters*
Vera Rosenerry, *Vera's First Day of School*
David Shannon, *No, David!* (also *David Goes to School* and *David Gets In Trouble*)
Kathy Stinson, *Red is Best*

CONNECT: (FOR 2–3)

Diana Cain Blumenthal, *I'm Not Invited*
Janan Cain, *The Way I Feel*
Eugenie Fernandes, *A Difficult Day*
Florence Parry Heide, *Some Things Are Scary*
Kevin Henkes, *Chester's Way* (or any book by Kevin Henkes)
Rebecca Jones, *Matthew and Tilly*

Norton Juster, *Hello, Good-bye Window*
Lisa Kopelke, *The Younger Brother's Survival Guide*
Alexis O'Neill, *The Recess Queen*
Todd Parr, *It's Okay to Be Different*
Barbara Reid, *The Party*
David Shannon, *No, David!* (also *David Goes to School* and *David Gets In Trouble*)
Bernard Waber, *Courage*

QUESTION

Barbara Abercrombie, *Charlie Anderson*
Louise Borden, *The Day Eddie Met the Author*
Eve Bunting, *Fly Away Home*
Timothy Basil Ering, *The Story of Frog Belly Rat Bone*
Dennis Haseley, *A Story for Bear*
Oliver Jeffers, *Lost and Found*
Paul Owen Lewis, *The Jupiter Stone*
Lois Rock, *I Wonder Why*
Eric Rohmann, *The Cinder-Eyed Cats*
Eric Rohmann, *Clara and Asha*
William Steig, *Sylvester and the Magic Pebble*

VISUALIZE

John Burningham, *Seasons*
Jan Carr, *Splish, Splash, Spring!*
Marie Hall Ets, *Gilberto and the Wind*
Patricia Hubbell, *Sidewalk Trip*
Ezra Jack Keats, *The Snowy Day*
Jonathon London, *Puddles*
Lynn Plourde, *Wild Child* (also *Winter Waits, Spring's Sprung, Summer's Vacation*)
Pam Munoz Ryan, *Hello Ocean*
Joanne Ryder, *Snail's Spell*
George David Weiss, *What A Wonderful World*

INFER

Jez Alborough, *Hug*
Keith Baker, *Little Green*
Suzanne Bloom, *A Splendid Friend, Indeed*
Anthony Browne, *Willy the Wizard* (or any of the Willy books)
Alexander Day, *Good Dog Carl*
Mem Fox, *Tough Boris*
Barbara Lahman, *Museum Trip*
Popov, *Why?*

Chris Raschka, *Yo! Yes!*
Peter Sis, *Madlenka's Dog*
Chris Van Allsburg, *The Sweetest Fig*
David Wiesner, *Tuesday*
Jeanette Winter, *Mama* (plus Isabella Hatkoff, *Owen and Mzee*)
Ed Young, *Seven Blind Mice*

TRANSFORM

John Burningham, *Hey! Get Off Our Train*
Barbara Cooney, *Miss Rumphius*
Julie Danneberg, *First Day Jitters*
Denise Fleming, *Where Once There Was a Wood*
Mem Fox, *Whoever You Are*
Patrick McDonnell, *The Gift of Nothing*
David McPhail, *The Teddy Bear*
Emily Pearson, *Ordinary Mary's Extraordinary Deed*
Peter Reynolds, *The Dot*
Peter Reynolds, *Ish*
Amy Krouse Rosenthal, *Cookies: Bite-Size Life Lessons*
James Simon, *My Friend Whale*
Shelley Moore Thomas, *Somewhere Today: A Book of Peace*
Melanie Watt, *Scaredy Squirrel*

Top Picks for Reading Power (Intermediate/Secondary)

CONNECT

Paul Fleischmann, *Rondo in C*
Florence Parry Heide, *Some Things Are Scary*
Lisa Kopelke, *The Younger Brother's Survival Guide*
Tom Lichtenheld, *What Are You So Grumpy About?*
Colin McNaughton, *Once Upon An Ordinary School Day*
Alexis O'Neill, *The Recess Queen*
Patricia Polacco, *My Rotten Red-Headed Older Brother*
David Shannon, *No, David!* (also *David Goes to School* and *David Gets In Trouble*)
Shaun Tan, *The Red Tree*
Judith Viorst, *If I Were In Charge of the World* (poetry)
Bernard Waber, *Courage*

QUESTION

Barbara Abercrombie, *Charlie Anderson*
Pat Bisson, *The Summer My Father Was Ten*
Eve Bunting, *Fly Away Home*
Eve Bunting, *Gleam and Glow*
Jennifer Riesmeyer Elvgren, *Josias, Hold the Book*
Paul Owen Lewis, *The Jupiter Stone*

Sarah Perry, *If*
Christopher Phillips, *The Philosopher's Club*
Allan Say, *The Stranger in the Mirror*
Frances Thomas, *Mr. Bear and the Bear*
Ian Wallace, *Boy of the Deeps*

VISUALIZE

Lewis Carroll, *Jabberwocky*
Dominique Demers, *Every Single Night*
Sheree Fitch, *No Two Snowflakes*
Jimmy Liao, *The Sound of Colors*
Sheryl McFarlane, *Jessie's Island*
Dav Pilkey, *The Paperboy*
Lynn Plourde, *Wild Child* (also *Winter Waits, Spring's Sprung, Summer's Vacation*)
Pam Munoz Ryan, *Hello Ocean*
Cynthia Rylant, *In November*
Stephanie St. Pierre, *What the Sea Saw*
Sarah Thomson, *Imagine a Day*
Sarah Thomson, *Imagine a Night*
Valerie Worth, *All the Small Poems* (poetry)
Charlotte Zolotow, *The Seashore Book*

Anthony Browne, *The Piggybook*

Anthony Browne, *Voices in the Park*

Roberto Innocenti, *Rose Blanche*

Barbara Lahman, *The Red Book* and *Museum Trip*

James Marshall, *George and Martha*

Popov, *Why?*

Chris Raschka, *Ring! Yo!*

Chris Raschka, *Yo! Yes!*

Chris Van Allsburg, *The Mysteries of Harris Burdick*

Chris Van Allsburg, *The Sweetest Fig* (anything by Chris Van Allsburg!)

David Wiesner, *June 29, 1999* (anything by David Wiesner)

Margaret Wild, *Fox*

Jeanette Winter, *Mama* (plus Isabella Hatkoff, *Owen and Mzee*)

Byrd Baylor, *The Table Where Rich People Sit*

Eve Bunting, *Riding the Tiger*

John Burningham, *Oi! Get off Our Train*

Jane Cutler, *The Cello of Mr. O*

Sarah Kilborne, *Peach and Blue*

Madonna, *Mr. Peabody's Apples*

Patrick McDonnell, *The Gift of Nothing*

Jon Muth, *The Three Questions*

Jon Muth, *Zen Shorts*

Emily Pearson, *Ordinary Mary's Extraordinary Deed*

Peter Reynolds, *The Dot*

Peter Reynolds, *Ish*

Sam Swope, *The Araboolies of Liberty Street*

Shaun Tan, *The Red Tree*

Melanie Watt, *Scaredy Squirrel*

Margaret Wild, *Fox*

Troy Wilson, *Perfect Man*

Creating a Book Bin Collection

I always stress in workshops that creating Book Bins for your school is not a necessity; however, they do make things easier for teachers. The success of this program is not tied to the specific book titles provided, but is strategy-driven. As teachers, most of us have our own collection of books that accumulates each year. Reading Power collections can begin simply with your own personal collections. School Libraries are also invaluable resources for gathering material.

Part of what makes Reading Power unique among comprehension teaching programs is its tie to the literature; part of what makes Reading Power unique to individual teachers is the books they choose to model and practise with their students. Teachers will need to look for the most appropriate books for their particular school culture—as well as for the age and interests of their students—to add to their own Book Bin collections. Adding your own favorites to the Book Bins will increase your and your students' interest and understanding of each Reading Power.

To get started on your collection, here are some tips:

- Use the booklists at the end of each section as your starting point. You DO NOT need to purchase all the books on the list, but try to select a few from each heading to ensure a variety of topics in each bin.
- Books for Modeling (Gem-bag books): three to four books for each reading power to be used by the teachers only
- Books for Independent Practice: ideally enough for one per student or one for a pair of students (15–30 books)
- These books are not leveled, but try to include books for a range of reading abilities.
- One Bin of books costs between $300 to $400, depending on how smart a shopper you are and if the books are hard or soft cover.

We found that a plastic tub with a snap lid made an excellent Book Bin. We labeled each tub with the name of the strategy and taped a list of the titles to the inside of the lid, so that teachers could keep track of the books in that Bin. Each book was labeled with a strategy code: *C* for Connect, *Q* for Question, etc.

- Each Bin should have a list of books inside—taped to the inside cover or loose in the bottom of the Bin—so that teachers can do a quick inventory before returning or passing it on to another teacher
- Bins should have lids so that they can be stored more easily.
- Each Bin should be clearly labeled with the Reading Power strategy.
- Bins should be kept in a central location with some type of sign-out system, so that teachers know where to find them.

If your school does decide to create Reading Power Book Bins, here are some suggestions of ways to find the best sources in your area:

- Scholastic Book Fairs and monthly Book Clubs
- Public Libraries often hold yearly book sales where you can get picture books in decent condition for very reasonable prices.
- Used bookstores —always treasures waiting to be discovered!
- Chapters.Indigo.ca, Amazon.com, Barnesandnoble.com, etc.
- Google search for used bookstores if you are looking for a particular title (www.alibris.com or www.abebooks.com are both great resources for finding used books)
- Don't forget garage and church sales, local bookstores, and warehouse sales in larger centres.

If your school decides not to create Reading Power Book Bins, here are some alternatives:

Wendy Cameron, teacher-librarian at Wolfe Elementary, has created Reading Power bookshelves in her library so teachers can easily locate books for each strategy.

- Use the school library.
- Have a teacher-librarian pull the books and create shelves for each Reading Power strategy.
- Have a teacher-librarian label the spines of appropriate books with *C, Q, V, I,* and/or *T* for each reading power, so that teachers and students can locate them quickly.
- Go to a public library with a Reading Power booklist and take out enough books to create a temporary bin in your classroom.
- Use your own classroom book collection and label the appropriate books with the Reading Power strategy.

Reading Power Instruction

Modeling

I always tell teachers at my workshops that they don't really need the Reading Powers Model and don't really need Reading Power Book Bins. What is essential to the success of this program is their direct teaching.

We have two voices—a speaking voice and a thinking voice. The thinking voice, that voice in your head, is what good readers pay attention to when they are reading to help them make better sense of the text.

We can never assume that students comprehend their own inner voice of understanding. The Reading Powers Model helps answer the question, "What does thinking look like?" but only the teacher can help answer the question, "What does thinking *sound* like?" If we want to help our students become better readers, we need to show them what a good reader looks like, sounds like, and thinks like (Stephanie Harvey demonstrates this brilliantly in her videos). I try to model it when I give workshops. It is not difficult to do, and some teachers are more comfortable doing it than others, but once students see and hear their teacher reading out loud and thinking out loud, comprehension becomes a tangible, concrete experience for them.

I went to university at a time when Whole Language was the rage. I learned to become a "facilitator" and an "observer" in the classroom. I learned how to assess using a variety of checklists and how to meet the needs of my students by working with small groups and teaching on an "as the need arises" basis. I don't remember learning how to do a great deal of direct teaching, nor do I remember having sponsor teachers who did a lot of explicit instruction.

When I taught my five-year-old son how to tie his shoe laces, I did not do it by telling him how. I *showed* him how—not just once, but many, many times. Then he tried to do it himself and he practised—not just once, but many, many times. A new skill, whether it be tying shoes or reading with meaning, needs to be taught in the same way.

I explain to my students:

> We have two voices: a speaking voice and a thinking voice. A speaking voice is the voice people hear when we talk. A thinking voice is the voice inside our heads that other people can't hear. When we read silently and our speaking voice is quiet, our thinking voice needs to be very, very loud.

Teachers have many opportunities in their day to model their thinking. It does not need to be in a formal lesson, but I encourage you to find moments in your read-alouds, guided reading, or whole-class reading where you can stop reading and simply say, "When I read this part, I started to think about…"

Thinking needs to be made visible and concrete, and there are different ways to illustrate this. Sticky notes stuck directly onto the pages while you read can mark your "thinking voice." John Dyer, a primary teacher at Southlands Elementary School, has a wonderful method of showing his students when he is using his thinking voice. He attaches a large white cutouts of a Talking bubble and a Thinking bubble to rulers (see templates on page 33). Each time he reads from a book with his speaking voice, he holds up the Talking bubble. Each time he is explaining what his thinking voice is saying, he switches and holds up his Thinking bubble.

It is that thinking voice that helps a reader make sense of what they are reading. During all my modeling lessons when I first introduce a new strategy, I explain to the students exactly what I am going to be doing:

> Today I'm going to be reading this story out loud and using my speaking voice. But every time my thinking voice makes a connection (or asks a question, or makes a picture in my head, etc.) I'm going to stop reading and tell you what I'm thinking. It is called a "read-aloud/think-aloud."

I have had teachers tell me that these read-aloud/think-alouds take a long time. Yes, they do. They take much longer than simply reading a story. But I strongly believe that it is time well spent. It is important to take this time when introducing a strategy. Remind yourself that you are not going to be reading aloud this way forever—you are simply showing your students how to "tie their shoelaces." If you don't show them, they will eventually trip over the pages of their texts with little or no understanding.

Some teachers have expressed concern over the "distraction" this can cause to their reading. Is it distracting to have to stop every few pages to tell your class what you are thinking about? Yes, it can be. But remember the point of the lesson. It is not my intention to ask students questions about the content of the text after I finish reading: the intention of this lesson is to model my thinking.

"I argue with myself, you're telling stories and you're supposed to be teaching. I am teaching. Storytelling is teaching."
— Frank McCourt, *Teacher Man*

Once students see what you are doing, they inevitably want to participate. This will end up taking too much time. It is important for students to know that, while you are modeling, it is your turn:

For the next few days I'm going to be *modeling my thinking*. When I'm modeling, it means that it is my turn to share my thinking voice.

One way we solved this problem was the "quiet connections thumbs-up" system—if children make a connection while you're reading, they can participate by showing you their thumbs-up without interrupting your modeling lesson. This works for the most part, except for the occasional student who continues to wave double thumbs up in huge circles in front of your face while you read! A teacher told me at a workshop that she was substituting in a Kindergarten class and, while she was reading, the students all started making strange "donkey ear" gestures on their heads. Surprised by this strange reaction, she asked them what they were doing. "We're making connections," one student explained. "This is our brain moving!"

Four Components of Reading Instruction

1. Teacher Modeling

explicit teaching, demonstrating, reading aloud/thinking aloud, "thinking voice–speaking voice"

2. Guided Practice

teacher and students practising together in large or small groups

3. Independent Practice

students trying on their own, with monitoring

4. Application

to real reading and writing experiences

Intentionally integrating the language of reading and thinking into your classroom is essential to helping your students become strategic thinkers.

The chart of the Four Components of Comprehension Instruction is based on David Pearson's model of "gradually releasing responsibility" to students. Each of the four components is important, but none more important than stage 1, Teacher Modeling. Repeated modeling of your thinking while you read aloud to teach each new strategy is essential. We should never assume that children have ever heard "that voice" inside their heads while they read. They need to see and hear your inner voice while you read in order to be able to activate their own.

Teachers will often ask, "How many times do I need to model?" When you are first introducing one of Reading Powers, it is essential that you model your thinking explicitly with at least two or three different books over two or three different days. After that, continue to model your thinking when you read, but not to the extent that you would during those first introductory lessons, pausing only once or twice to share your thinking, rather than throughout the book. I remember clearly the first year I was teaching Reading Power. I had been modeling Connecting for several weeks. The children were very polite as I paused repeatedly during my lengthy read-alouds to share the parts of my life that the story reminded me of. After several days and many modeling lessons, little Christian put up his hand and said, "Ah, Miss Gear—we get it." Perhaps I had made the "gradual release of responsibility" a little too gradual, but I would rather have one "we get it" than twenty "I don't get it"s.

"Conversation is a basis for critical thinking. It is the thread that ties together cognitive strategies and provides students with the practice that becomes the foundation for reading, writing, and thinking."
— Ann Ketch, *The Reading Teacher*, 59:1

In the second stage, Guided Practice, students need time to work in a whole-class or small-group setting, with the teacher still guiding them and using the language of the strategy. These strategies can also be reinforced during your guided reading lessons. In the Independent Practice stage, the children are ready to work through the strategy on their own with their own book. During this guided practice stage, it is important for teachers to provide opportunities for students to share their thinking with each other. Discussion helps children sort out their ideas and strengthens their understanding, helping to make their ideas more concrete. Understanding evolves from conversation.

Finally, our goal for anything we teach is that the students will be able to apply what they learn in all reading situations. A couple extreme examples of Application occurred during that first year of teaching Reading Power. The first was Carmen, who was in Grade 3 at Laura Secord. Her class had spent the past several weeks working on making connections. One afternoon, while she was reading one of the books she had just borrowed from the library, she quietly went to her teacher with a puzzled look on her face and asked, "Am I allowed to make a Connection with a library book?" Clearly, she hadn't grasped the concept of Application! Then there was Calvin, a little boy in Grade 1 who, while listening to a story in the library, began waving his hand furiously in the air. "Calvin," the teacher-librarian asked, "Do you need to go to the bathroom?" "NO!" Calvin shouted, "I'M HAVING A CONNECTION!"

Components of Reading Power Instruction

Because of the importance of explicit teaching in this approach, I have used it as a framework to present a general outline of what Reading Power instruction might look like in a classroom:

1. Teacher Modeling (week 1)

- Introduce the new reading power and use the Reading Powers Model (page 20) to emphasize the objective of becoming good readers.
- Use the phrase "good readers " as much as possible for each specific reading power.
- From the Gem bag, select one book per day for three to five days (depending on the grade and students' experience with the strategy) for your modeling.
- Read the Gem aloud: as you read, stop and tell students what you are thinking.
- Use sticky notes to write your thoughts, connections, questions, etc., sticking them directly into the book wherever you stop.
- Begin to code your notes with specific Reading Power codes.

2. Guided Practice (week 2)

- Select a book from the Book Bin to use in guided practice in a whole class or small group. Read the story aloud, but instead of giving your insights and thoughts, ask the students for theirs.
- Pass out sticky notes and, as you read, ask for students to come up and stick their notes in the book to indicate connections, questions, etc.
- Encourage the students to use the codes you modeled.
- Support the students, giving feedback and encouraging discussions.
- Provide opportunities for the students to share their thinking with each other.
- Reinforce strategy during guided reading lessons.

Sequential Lessons for Connecting:
page 37
Sequential Lessons for Questioning:
page 53
Sequential Lessons for Visualizing:
page 68
Sequential Lessons for Inferring:
page 83
Sequential Lessons for Transforming:
page 101

3. Independent Practice (weeks 3–4)

- It is very important to continue modeling and guided practice each day.
- Individually or in pairs, students practise the reading power with sticky notes and books from the Bin.
- Sometimes students read-aloud/think-aloud with a partner; other times they read-silently/think-on-paper solo, then share with a partner.
- Come together to discuss and share ideas as a group or during individual conferences.
- Students can make their own charts, respond in journals or response logs, or use response sheets you provide to extend their thinking into writing.

Talking and Thinking Bubble Templates

Name: _____ Date: _____

Talking

Thinking

3   The Power to Connect

Connect Song
(to the tune of "Brush Your Teeth")

When I read a story and my brain says, "Hey!
This part reminds me of the other day!"
It's called "connect"—da da da da da da da da da
It's called "connect"—da da da da da da da da da

When I read a story and my brain says, "Whoa!
This part reminds me of my friend, Jo!"
It's called "connect"—da da da da da da da da da
It's called "connect"—da da da da da da da da da

When I read a story and my brain says, "Cool!
This part reminds me of my school!"
It's called "connect"—da da da da da da da da da
It's called "connect"—da da da da da da da da da

When I read a story and my brain says "Look!
This part reminds me of another book!"
It's called "connect"—da da da da da da da da da
It's called "connect"—da da da da da da da da da

When I read a story and my brain says, "Wow!
This part reminds me of my grandpa's cow!"
It's called "connect"—da da da da da da da da da
It's called "connect"—da da da da da da da da da

✳ ✳ ✳

"No story sits by itself. Sometimes stories meet at corners and sometimes they cover one another completely, like stones beneath a river."
— Mitch Albom, *The Five People You Meet in Heaven*

I am in a book club. At the end of our monthly meetings, after rich and thoughtful discussions about the books, after sharing passages that affected us or images that stayed with us, after analyzing the writers' craft, there are some books I may "accidentally" leave behind. There are other books I bring home, but then happily pass on to my sister or a friend to read without worrying about getting them back. But there are a certain few books are brought home from book club and placed on a special shelf on the bookcase in my living room. There they are, not to be read by anyone else—but to sit and be coveted. I touch their spines every once in a while—I may even flip through the pages—but those books have become my treasures. Why, I often wondered, did some books end up on this shelf and not others? Children often say they like a particular book because "it was good." Perhaps that actually means, "I connected to this book." I now understand that the books that end up on my shelf are there because my life story has somehow been woven into their pages. Those books are no longer someone else's story—they have become my story.

The ability to connect to text is perhaps the easiest one for children to understand and master, yet it is singularly the most powerful. Connecting creates the path for all other reading strategies to walk upon. When a reader begins to relate to a story in terms of his or her own life, the story simply makes more sense. We know ourselves better than we know anything else, so to read a book through the eyes of our own lives is the essence of "creating meaning." The notion that we bring ourselves into the books we read, that we weave our life stories into the stories that we read, is a deep truth. To teach children to learn to make sense of a text for themselves is teaching them not *what* to think, but *how* to think. When we teach children to connect, we are teaching them to pay attention to moments, feelings, characters, and places in a story which trigger links to their own feelings, characters, and places in their life story. Reading unlocks the memories that are the backdrop of our lives.

After a *Reading Power* workshop, a teacher came up to me to thank me for helping her solve one of the greatest mysteries of her life: why she has never liked borrowing books from the library. She explained that she had always been an avid reader, that reading books had been a hobby of hers all her life. She had, she was sometimes ashamed to admit, spent a small fortune on books. Friends and colleagues always wondered why she didn't just go to the library to borrow books to read instead of buying so many. But she had never, she told me, enjoyed borrowing books from the library. She had tried, but preferred instead to buy them. She never knew the reason for this, she said, until she heard me talk about connecting. She realized that, when she reads a book, the book becomes "her story" and that after experiencing the power of connecting through reading it, returning it to the library meant sharing her life with the next person who might come along and borrow that book. An extreme example perhaps, but one that clearly illustrates the power of connecting.

> "Your life is a story—it's just not written down on paper."

> "The words on the page are only half the story. The rest is what you bring to the party."—Toni Morrison, *The Reader as Artist*

When readers learn to connect when reading:

- the story reminds them of something they have experienced.
- their minds become flooded with memories.
- they are making sense of the text in terms of events and people in their own lives.
- they can make connections to pictures, plot, characters, and feelings from the story.
- they are most likely reading books about real-life situations, such as family, friendship, school, siblings, pets, vacations, etc.

Introducing the Power to Connect

When introducing the strategy of connecting, I like to tell the children something that I believe:

> My life is a story and your life is a story. They may not be written down on paper but, nevertheless, they are stories. Let's pretend for a moment that I did write my story down on paper. How big would it be?

(I hold my hands to show the thickness of my imaginary book)

It might be this big. And what would be in this life story? Well, in my life story will be everything I've done, places I've been to, adventures I had, people I've met, things that I've learned. Are all the chapters in my life story happy? Will some be sad? Surprising? Funny? What about if my grandmother, who died when she was 93, wrote her life story down on paper—how big would her book be? What about if you're in Grade 7? What about if you are in Kindergarten? If you are in Kindergarten, your life story might not very big right now—but everything you do in your life, you add another chapter.

(Show different book sizes with hands.)

In real life, people don't usually write their entire life stories down on paper— so where do they keep them? In a desk? Under the bed? Where? Our life stories are stored in this amazing place called the brain. Now my brain is probably about this big.

(Show with hands.)

Isn't it amazing to think that my whole life story is stored in that small place? When we read, something remarkable happens: something from the story in the book can trigger a memory from the story in our lives. When this happens, it is connecting—the joining together of two stories, one from the text and one from our lives.

Our life experiences deepen and enrich our life story to create the "well of experiences" from which we draw when we read. Unfortunately not all children come to us with a lot of life stories upon which to draw. We need to be aware of this and try to provide stories they will be able to connect with successfully: stories about school, family, friendship, siblings, losing a tooth, birthday parties, pets. We need to be constantly modeling our own connections and allowing children to share theirs. Just as we do not connect to every book we read, we cannot expect our students to connect to every book. If a child does not connect to a story one day, it's okay. Encourage the child to connect to the next story. We can gently nudge children in the direction we want them to go by continually modeling our thinking and encouraging them to become more confident in their connections. Viviane, a Grade 2 student at Laura Secord, was a keen Connecter. During the Group Connect lessons (see page 38), she was one of the first to put her sticky note in the book. But after reading the story *Franklin's New Friend* to the class, Viviane was the only student who still had her sticky in her hand. When I questioned why she hadn't added her sticky to the book, she responded, "How can I make a connection to that book? I am NOT a turtle!"

An important thing to make children aware of is the individuality that comes from making sense of text. Books like *Rondo in C* or *Once Upon an Ordinary School Day* illustrate this point well. After reading one of those books, I always ask the students this important question: "Why is it that everyone in the room is listening to the same piece of music (or reading the same story) but they are all thinking of different things? Why isn't everyone thinking of the same thing?" Children very quickly are able to tell me the answer: Because we are all different.

When discussing where our "life story is stored," remind students that memories are also stored in our hearts. Connections tied to feelings and emotions are often more powerful and meaningful than those which are not.

"You know and understand yourself better than anyone else, so if you can learn to put yourself into the stories you read it will help you to understand them much better."

"There is no right or wrong way to make a connection. Every person's life story is filled with different memories because our life stories are all different. When we read, we are all going to be connecting to different things in the story because we are all different."

> "If books could have more, give more, be more, show more, they would still need readers, who bring to them sound and smell and light and all the rest that can't be in books. The book needs you."
> — Gary Paulson, *The Winter Room*

And because we are all different and the stories of our lives are all different, we are all going to make different connections to the books we read. There is no one right way to connect, and what triggers a memory for one person may not trigger a memory for anybody else. On the other hand, two people might make a connection to the same part of the story for completely different reasons. Helping children understand that there is no one right way to connect is the first step towards their understanding that their own experiences and knowledge, above everything else, are what is going to help them make sense of what they are reading.

Connecting is one of the easiest strategies for children to grasp. We need to be careful, however, that we are guiding students to make connections that are meaningful. While it may be easy to look at a picture of a dog and say, "My uncle has a dog," that is not elevating our students' thinking or understanding. It is up to us to guide our students towards making connections that are going to move them forward in their thinking.

Sequential Lessons for Connecting

Lesson 1 (Teacher Directed): Introducing the Power

- See "Introducing the Power to Connect" on page 35.
- Read *Rondo in C* by Paul Fleischman or *Once Upon an Ordinary School Day* by Colin McNaughton
- Ask the students, "Why is it, in this book, when everyone in the room was listening to the same piece of music, everyone was thinking of something different?"
- Discuss the fact that, even though everyone was listening to the same music, each person was thinking about different things because each person has a different "life story" or different experiences.
- Discuss that this is the same thing that happens when we read—everyone makes different connections because everyone has a different life, different memories, and different experiences stored in our powerful brains. Explain that the story of your life what will help you understand the story you are reading.

Lessons 2–3 (Teacher Directed): Modeling Your Thinking

- Find a picture book that elicits strong connections and memories for you.
- Model a read-aloud/think-aloud with this special Connect book, using sticky notes to mark your connections with a *C* for Connect or an *R* for "Reminds me of." Pause on a page, insert your sticky note, and model using this language: "This part of the story reminds me of…"
- Students wishing to participate while you are modeling can do so with a "quiet connection thumbs-up" (see page 30).
- Follow with at least two more similar lessons using books from the Gem bag. As you model, try to make sure that you are connecting to each of these: a part of the story, a picture, a character, and a feeling.

My special Connect book, the one I always use to model that first Connect lesson, is Robert McKlosky's *One Morning in Maine* because it reminds me of summer holidays spent with my family on Mayne Island. The story is filled with so many fond memories of my childhood, it feels as if it was written about me. One teacher who was born in Saskatchewan uses *If You're Not From the Prairie* by Henry Ripplinger. It takes her two days to read because each page is a story from her childhood on the farm. Jodi Carson, a Literacy Mentor, searched for weeks until she finally found her Connect book: *Tales of a Gambling Grandma* by David Kaur Khalsa, because it reminds her of when her grandmother used to teach her and her sister how to play blackjack every Friday night. It may take you a few visits to the library to find your own Connect book—but when you do, it makes that first lesson a powerful one. The students may not remember the story you read, but they certainly will remember the story you tell.

Grade 2 Sample

Lesson 4 (Guided Group Practice): Group Connect

- Read aloud a book from the Connect Bin and have students listen for all their connections.
- Read the book again, and have each student come up and put one sticky note (with the student's name on it) on the page where the best connection was made, or where the student's thinking voice "was the loudest." They are not sharing at this point, simply placing their sticky notes in the book when you get to the right page.
- Continue to model by placing your own sticky note.
- Model how you want students to share: "I put my sticky on the page where…. This reminded me of…."
- Invite students to share their connections out loud with a partner. When partners are sharing, circulate the room, listening for all connections. Choose one pair of students to come up to the front to model their connections. Choose the pair who really went beyond a simple statement like "This reminds me of my brother" to sharing a "chapter" of their life stories.

You can follow this lesson with similar Group Connects, and have students share a connection afterwards with a partner. Choose one or two pairs to model their connections for the class.

Connecting to feelings is often the most challenging because feelings are often inferred, so this is something that you could model.

This same lesson could be done when introducing other ways we can make connections to books (see Expanding Your Connections #2 on page 46):

Text-to-Self: "This book reminds me of something that happened to me."

Text-to-Text: "This book reminds me of another book I've read."

Text-to-World: "This book reminds me of something that doesn't just affect me personally, but affects other people in the world (e.g., bullying)."

- Suggested books for this lesson: *Some Things Are Scary* by Florence Pam Heide, *Courage* by Bernard Waber, and *The Party* by Barbara Reid.

Lessons 5–6 (Guided Group Practice): Expanding Connections

- Create a large chart (Expanding Your Connections #1 on page 45) to display in the classroom.
- Explain to students that, when we read, we can connect to different parts of the book: part of the story, a picture, a character, or a feeling.
- Repeat Group Connect lesson (page 38). After students have placed their stickies in the book, explain that you will be returning their stickies shortly. Refer to the chart and tell them you would like the stickies placed on the column where they think they made their connection today. Model with your sticky note and explain your thinking.
- Page by page, pass the stickies back and have students put them onto the chart.
- The next day, remind students where they put their stickies on the chart. Encourage them to try to put their stickies in a different spot today during the Group Connect.
- Introduce the idea of Quick Connections (My uncle has a dog like that) and Deep Thinking Connections (That reminds me of the time when I got teased at school for wearing dresses every day and I felt really embarrassed). Spend time modeling the difference between these two, so that students can begin to expand their thinking.

Grade 1 Sample

Lessons 7–9 (Independent Practice): Choosing a Book

Limit the number of sticky notes you give students according to the grade: a Grade 1 student might have three; a Grade 5 might have 6.

- Have each student choose his or own book from the Connect Bin. Provide each with their own sticky notes.
- Ask them to read silently and mark their connections with their sticky notes. Older students can jot down notes about their connections on each sticky; younger students will simply code the sticky with a *C* and their names.
- As students finish, they can find a partner and share their connections.
- This lesson works very well if, after students mark their connections, they trade books with a partner and mark their connections using different-colored sticky notes. Partners then get together to share and compare their connections.

Lessons 10–12 (Independent Practice): Expanding Connections Through Writing

Encourage students to find a page where both partners put a sticky note, but had different connections. These "double connection" pages can be shared with the class.

In terms of assessing, peeled-off sticky notes become invaluable as small windows into your students' thinking.

- Explain how each sticky note placed in a book represents a little chapter of a student's life.
- Model how to expand this into writing by choosing one of your previous connections and writing it out—with details, names, and feelings—on chart paper.
- After students read and mark their connections independently, have them choose the connection where their "thinking voice was the loudest" and expand this connection into writing. This could be done by writing about it in a journal, or using one of the templates (pages 47–50).
- Many teachers give students Reading Power Notebooks for these writing extensions. Students can peel the stickies from the book they read, stick them on one page of the notebook with title and author at the top, then choose one of the connections to write about on the opposite page.
- Rule: Never put a book back into the Book Bin and "leave your thinking behind." Sticky notes must be peeled off before a book is returned.

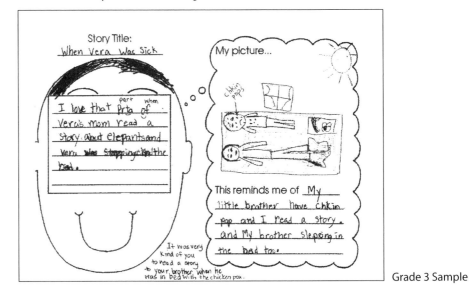

Grade 3 Sample

Lesson 13 (Independent Practice): Finding Your Own Connect Book

- Review the concept of the Connect power.
- Older students can be given the assignment of finding their own special Connect book in the school or public library.
  - Go to the library and search for your special "connect book".
  - Write about the picture book that you made strong connections with.
    1. Give a brief summary of the story
    2. Use examples that show how you connected to the book through the storyline, pictures, characters, or feelings.
    3. Explain whether you made T–S, T–T, T–W connections. Give examples.
    4. Explain what makes this book special to you.
  - Prepare an oral presentation for the class on your "Connect Book"
- Books can be displayed, along with the written connections and photo of the student.
- As teacher, you can participate in the display with your own Connect book.

Title: The Hockey Sweater

Author: Roch Carrier

Illustrator: Sheldon Cohen

The book I chose to be my special Connect book is *The Hockey Sweater* by Roch Carrier. It is the story of a boy who lives in a small town in Montreal. All the kids in the small town are crazy about hockey and they play hockey and think about hockey all day long. Their favorite team is the Montreal Canadiens and their favorite player is Maurice Richard. The boy ends up getting a new hockey jersey, but by mistake, it is a Toronto Maple Leafs jersey and not a Montreal Canadiens jersey. His mum makes him wear it anyways and his friends and the coach won't let him play.

I made a lot of connections to this book and through the character, storyline, and feelings. The main character really reminded me of my younger brother, Pete. Pete loved hockey and loved the Montreal Canadiens more than anything else. He, like the main character, would have been devastated if he had to wear a Toronto jersey. I also made connections to the storyline. The story showed how important hockey was to this town. Everybody was involved in hockey whether they were playing or listening to the game on the radio. This reminds me of growing up in the small town of Trail, BC, where everyone lived and loved hockey. I made connections to the feelings in the book. It reminded me of the intense feeling my brother showed when the Montreal Canadiens lost. When the main character broke his stick in frustration, it reminded me of my brother hitting the television when his favorite team lost—especially to the Toronto Maple Leafs.

I made T–S connections to this book and also T–W connections. The book reminded me of things in my own childhood and also it reminded me how a town or country can go crazy when their hockey team is winning or in the playoffs.

This book is my special Connect book because when I read it, it made me feel like I was reading about my own brother and my own town.

Lesson 14: Reflective Journal

Have students record their thoughts about this new strategy and what they've learned about connecting. "How has connecting while you read helped you to understand the story better? Show me or tell me about your thinking."

Connecting

When we learned connecting it was fun. I liked finding # parts of the story that felt like they were really about me. Like when we read "No David" and it was so funny and just like when I do stuff and my mom says, "No Matthew!" Connecting is cool and fun and helps keep my brain busy! busy! busy!

Other Connect Lessons

- Introduce students to different connect codes: T–S (Text-to-Self), T–T (Text-to-Text), T–W (Text-to-World). See chart on page 46.
- Have older students read a Connect book to their buddies and share connections.
- Have students make connections when reading library books.
- Have students and parents mark connections together in the same book when doing home reading or during student-led conferences.

Connect Booklist

Gems for Modeling Think-Alouds and Guided Practice

P = primary
I = intermediate
SR = social responsibility
A = Aboriginal

If we want our students to understand what connecting is, we need to show them what it looks like. Taking the time to model your thinking voice when introducing the power of Connecting is essential to their understanding. These books are for teachers to use when modeling read-aloud/think-alouds. Choose two or three from the list—each for a separate modeling lesson—and two or three for guided Group Connects (see page 38).

BOOKS ABOUT FAMILY/SIBLINGS

Blume, Judy. *The Pain and the Great One.* (I)
Gliori, Debi. *My Little Brother.* (P, I)
Hughes, Shirley. *The Trouble with Jack.* (P, I)
McPhail, David. *Sisters.* (P)
Polacco, Patricia. *My Rotten Red-Headed Older Brother.* (I)
Reid, Barbara. *The Party.* (P, I)

BOOKS ABOUT FEELINGS

Anholt, Catherine & Laurence. *Good Days, Bad Days.* (P)
Anholt, Catherine & Laurence. *What Makes Me Happy.* (P)
Cain, Janan. *The Way I Feel.* (P)
Carlson, Nancy. *There's a Big Beautiful World Out There!* (P)
Churchill, Vicki. *Sometimes I Like to Curl Up in a Ball.* (P).
Fernandes, Eugenie. *A Difficult Day.* (P)
Heide, Florence Parry. *Some Things Are Scary.* (P, I)
McLachlan, Patricia. *All the Places to Love.* (P, I)
Parr, Todd. *It's Okay to Be Different.* (SR) (P)
Waber, Bernard. *Courage.* (P, I)

BOOKS ABOUT FRIENDSHIP

Bourgeois, Paulette. *Franklin's Secret Club.* (P)
Cave, Kathryn. *That's What Friends Do.* (P)

Henkes, Kevin. *Chester's Way.* (P,I)
Jones, Rebecca. *Matthew and Tilly.* (SR) (I)
McBratney, Sam. *I'm Sorry.* (SR) (P)
Steig, William. *Amos and Boris.* (SR) (I)

LOSS OF LOVED ONE

Aliki. *The Two of Them.* (P, I)
DePaola, Tomie. *Nana Upstairs and Nana Downstairs.* (I)
Viorst, Judith. *The Tenth Good Thing about Barney.* (P, I)

MEMOIRS

Curtis, Jamie Lee. *When I Was Little: A Four Year Old's Memoir of Her Youth.* (P, I)
Rylant, Cynthia. *Birthday Presents.* (P, I)

BOOKS ABOUT SCHOOL

Ashley, Bernard. *Cleversticks.* (P)
Cox, Phil Roxbee. *Don't Be a Bully, Billy.* (P, I)
Fraser, Mary Ann. *I.Q. Goes to School.* (P, I)
Henkes, Kevin. *Lily's Purple Plastic Purse.* (P,I)
Lester, Helen. *Me First.* (SR) (P)
McNamara, Margaret. *The Playground Problem.* (SR) (P)
O'Neill, Alexis. *The Recess Queen.* (P, I)
Rathmann, Peggy. *Ruby the Copycat.* (P, I)
Rosenberry, Vera. *Vera's First Day of School.* (P)
Schwartz, Amy. *Things I Learned in Second Grade.* (P)
Simms, Laura. *Rotten Teeth.* (P, I)
Wells, Rosemary. *Timothy Goes to School.* (P, I)

SELF-IDENTITY, SELF-EXPRESSION

Browne, Anthony. *Things I Like.* (P)
Chodos-Irvine, Margaret. *Ella Sarah Gets Dressed.* (P)
DePaola, Tomie. *Oliver Button Is a Sissy.* (P, I)
Gilmor, Don. *When Vegetables Go Bad.* (P, I)

Heap, Sue. *Red Rockets and Rainbow Jelly.* (P)
Shannon, David. *David Gets in Trouble.* (P, I)
Shannon, David. *No, David!* (P, I)
Stinson, Kathy. *Red is Best.* (P)
Zolotow, Charlotte. *William's Doll.* (P, I)

Books for Independent Practice

P = primary
I = intermediate
SR = social responsibility
A = Aboriginal

Once students have seen you model connecting and have practised with the group, they are ready to choose their own books and practise making connections independently. Choose from the following books to create a collection of Connect books for your classroom. Be sure to include a variety of topics from the categories below.

BOOKS ABOUT FAMILY/SIBLINGS

Drucker, Malka. *Grandma's Latkes.* (I)
Edwards, Becky. *My Brother Sammy.* (P, I)
Gammell, Stephen. *Ride.* (I)
Henkes, Kevin. *Julius, Baby of the World.* (P, I)
Itaya, Atoshi. *Buttons and Bo.* (P) (SR)
Lewis, Rob. *Brothers and Sisters.* (P)
Little, Jean. *Emma's Yucky Brother.* (P, I)
Loewen, Iris. *My Kokum Called Today.* (P) (A)
Loyie, Larry. *As Long As the Rivers Flow.* (I) (A)
Numeroff, Laura. *What Mommies Do Best.* (P)
Numeroff, Laura. *What Daddies Do Best.* (P)
Plain, Ferguson. *Eagle Feather: An honour.* (P,I) (A)
Sears, Laurie. *Ian's Walk: A story about autism.* (I)
Stinson, Kathy. *Mom and Dad Don't Live Together Anymore.* (P, I)
Viorst, Judith. *The Good Bye Book.* (P, I)
Viorst, Judith. *Super-Completely and Totally the Messiest.* (P, I)

BOOKS ABOUT FRIENDSHIP

Austin, Margot. *A Friend for Growl Bear.* (P)
Bourgeois, Paulette. *Franklin Is Bossy.* (SR) (P)
Bourgeois, Paulette. *Franklin's New Friend.* (P)
Bourgeois, Paulette. *Franklin Plays the Game.* (P)
Champion, Joyce. *Emily and Alice, Best Friends.* (P, I)
Gardiner, Lindsey. *Not Fair, Won't Share!* (SR) (P)
Heine, Helme. *Friends.* (P)
Henkes, Kevin. *Chrysanthemum.* (P, I)
Henkes, Kevin. *A Weekend with Wendell.* (P, I)
Komaiko, Leah. *Earl's Too Cool for Me.* (P, I)
Ludwig, Trudy. *My Secret Bully.* (SR) (I)
Monson, A.M. *Wanted: Best Friend.* (P)
Oram, Haiwyn. *What's Naughty?* (P, I)
Rathman, Peggy. *Bootsie Barker Bites.* (SR) (P, I)

Rosen, Michael. *This Is Our House.* (P)
Snihura, Ulana. *I Miss Franklin P. Shuckles.* (P, I)
Viorst, Judith. *Rosie and Michael.* (P, I)
Zolotow, Charlotte. *The Unfriendly Book.* (SR) (I)

BOOKS ABOUT FEELINGS

Bang, Molly. *When Sophie Gets Angry.* (P, I)
Best, Cari. *Shrinking Violet.* (I)
Bourgeois, Paulette. *Franklin's Bad Day.* (P)
Carlson, Nancy. *I Like Me!* (P)
Einarson, Earl. *The Moccasins.* (P,I) (A)
Feiffer, Jules. *I Lost My Bear.* (P, I)
Gilmore, Rachna. *A Screaming Kind of Day.* (P, I)
Godwin, Patricia. *I Feel Orange Today.* (P)
Henkes, Kevin. *Wemberly Worried.* (P, I)
Hoelwarth, Cathryn Clinton. *The Underbed.* (P, I)
Hood, Susan. *Bad Hair Day.* (P)
Hunter, Jana Novotny. *I Have Feelings.* (P)
Lichtenheld, Tom. *What Are You So Grumpy About?* (P, I)
Monnier, Miriam. *Just Right.* (P)
Murphy, Joanne Brisson. *Feelings.* (I)
Rosenberry, Vera. *When Vera Was Sick.* (P, I)
Ruhmann, Karl. *But I Want To!* (P, I)
St. Anthony Catholic School Students. *When I'm Scared.* (P, I)
Dr. Seuss. *My Many Colored Days.* (P)
Stinson, Kathy. *Big or Little.* (P)
Viorst, Judith. *The Terrible, Horrible, No Good, Very Bad Day.* (P, I)
Wood, Audrey. *Quick as a Cricket.* (P)

LOSS OF LOVED ONE

London, Jonathon. *Liplap's Wish.* (P, I)
Wilhelm, Hans. *I'll Always Love You.* (P, I)

BOOKS ABOUT SCHOOL

Boelts, Maribeth. *When It's the Last Day of School.* (I)

Carlson, Nancy. *Loudmouth George and the Sixth-Grade Bully.* (SR) (I)

Cox, Phil Roxbee. *Give That Back, Jack!* (P, I)

DePaola, Tomie. *The Art Lesson.* (P, I)

Harris, Robie H. *I Am NOT Going to School Today.* (P)

Krensky, Stephen. *My Teacher's Secret Life.* (P, I)

Lasky, Kathryn. *Show and Tell Bunnies.* (P)

McDonald, Megan. *Insects Are My Life.* (SR) (P, I)

Allard, Harry G. *Miss Nelson Is Missing.* (P, I)

Naylor, Phyllis Reynolds. *King of the Playground.* (SR) (P, I)

Rogers, Jacqueline. *Tiptoe into Kindergarten.* (P)

Rylant, Cynthia. "Slower Than the Rest" in *Every Living Thing.* (I)

Schwartz, Amy. *Annabelle Swift, Kindergartner.* (P)

Shannon, David. *David Goes to School.* (P, I)

MEMOIRS

Bruchac, Joseph. *Fox Song.* (I) (A)

Fox, Mem. *Wilfred Gordon Macdonald Partridge.* (I)

Martin Jr., Bill. *Knots on a Counting Rope.* (I)

Rylant, Cynthia. *When I Was Young in the Mountains.* (P, I)

SELF-IDENTITY, SELF-EXPRESSION

Carrier, Roch. *The Hockey Sweater.* (P, I)

Beaumont, Karen. *I Like Myself.* (P)

Edwards, Becky. *My Cat Charlie.* (P, I)

Falconer, Ian. *Olivia.* (P, I)

Henkes, Kevin. *Owen.* (P, I)

Hoffman, Mary. *Amazing Grace.* (P, I)

Kraus, Robert. *Leo the Late Bloomer.* (P, I)

Lester, Helen. *Hooway for Wodney Wat.* (SR) (P)

Levine, Ellen. *I Hate English.* (P, I)

Lishak, Anthony. *Marlene's Magic Birthday.* (P, I)

Little, Jean. *Hey World, Here I Am!* (I)

McCloskey, Robert. *One Morning in Maine.* (P, I)

Moss, Miriam. *Wibble Wobble.* (P)

Sanderson, Esther. *Two Pairs of Shoes.* (P,I) (A)

Tibo, Gilles. *Shy Guy.* (P, I)

Viorst, Judith. *Earrings.* (P, I)

Viorst, Judith. *If I Were in Charge of the World and Other Worries.* (I)

Waber, Bernard. *Ira Sleeps Over.* (P, I)

Wallace, Ian. *Chin Chang and the Dragon's Dance.* (I)

Wallace, John. *Tiny Rabbit Goes to a Birthday Party.* (P)

Wells, Rosemary. *Shy Charles.* (P)

Zonta, Pat. *Jessica's X-Ray.* (P, I)

Expanding Your Connections #1

Name: _____   Date: _____

Connecting to…

the story	a picture	a character	a feeling

Expanding Your Connections #2

Name: _____ Date: _____

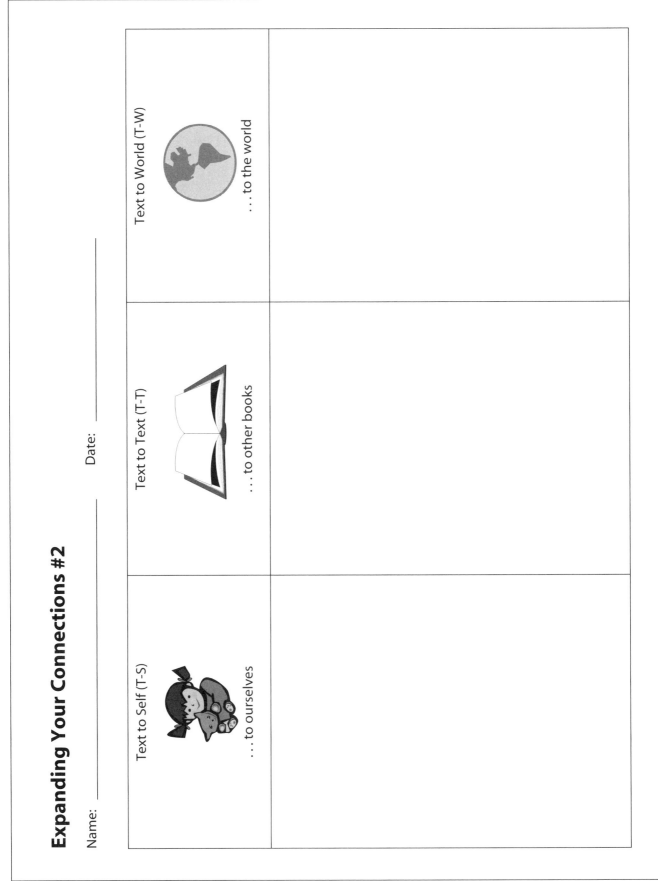

Text to Self (T-S)	Text to Text (T-T)	Text to World (T-W)
. . . to ourselves	. . . to other books	. . . to the world

Connecting Stories

Name: _____   Date: _____

Story Title: _____

Story   My Life

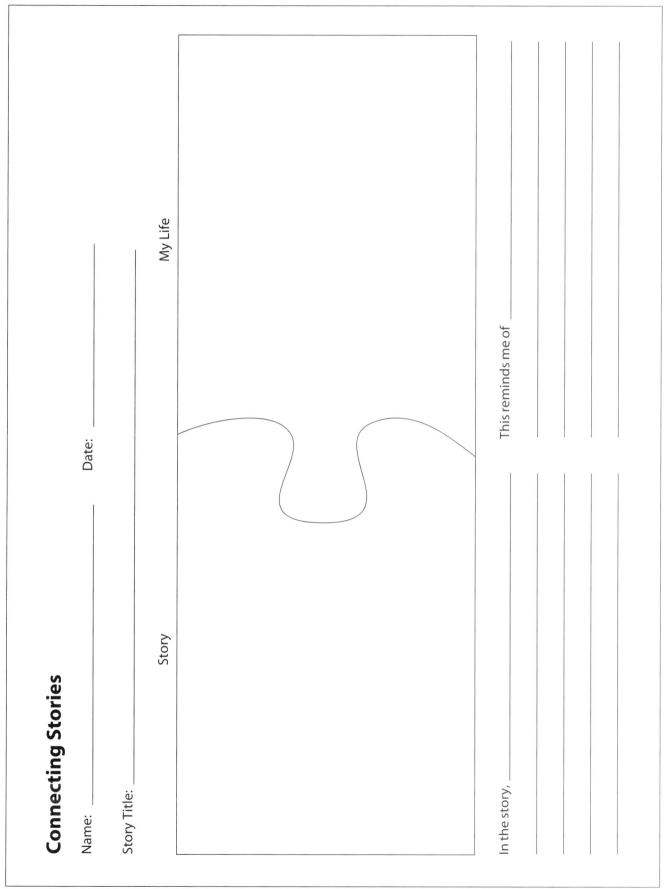

In the story, _____   This reminds me of _____

Making Connections #1

Name: _____   Date: _____

Title: _____   Author: _____

This part of the story reminds me of . . . .

_____

_____

_____

_____

Making Connections #2

Name: _____

Date: _____

Story Title: _____

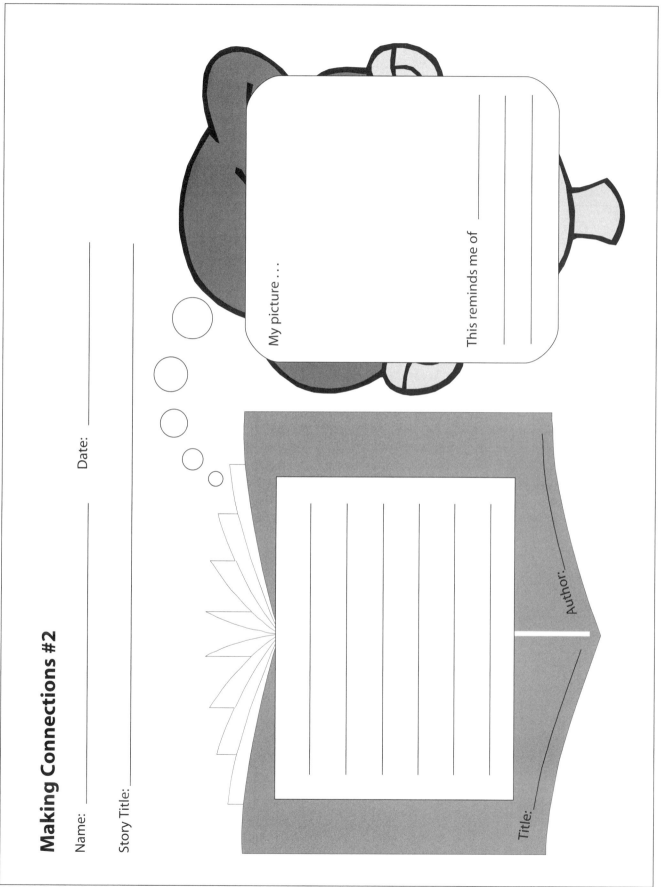

My picture . . .

This reminds me of _____

Title: _____

Author: _____

Making Connections #3

Name: _____   Date: _____

> **Good readers** make **connections** with what they are reading. When we read a story, it will remind each of us of different things. This **reminding** is also called *connecting*. Reading makes us think about something that has happened in our lives.

Title: _____

Author: _____

The **connections** I made…

_____

_____

_____

_____

_____

_____

_____

_____

_____

_____

_____

4 The Power to Question

Question Song
(to the tune of "Oh My Darling, Clementine")

Chorus:
Oh I wonder,
Oh I wonder,
Oh I wonder while I read.
All good readers ask deep questions
And they wonder while they read.

Sometimes when I ask a question
And I turn the page to look,
I find the answer to my question
And it's right there in the book.

But sometimes I can't find the answer
Even when the story's read.
So I have to find the answer
To the question—in my head!

(Repeat Chorus)

✳ ✳ ✳

When I was in Grade 7, we had "reading" twice a week. Reading in my class was working through an SRA kit—that wonderful compact neatly-organized box filled with shiny color-coded cards. Each card had a narrow black and white drawing at the top and the story below, followed by ten questions on the back. The stories were leveled by colors and we worked our way methodically through each of the stories of one color and then moved into the next set of colors. If my memory serves me correctly, the colors at the front of the box, at the lowest reading level, were muddy tones with rather unpleasant names: tan, rust, gray, mustard. The colors towards the back of the box were far more appealing: magenta, aquamarine, goldenrod.

Reading on Tuesday and Thursday afternoons looked like this: One row at a time, we each would go up to the SRA kit and select our card. I returned to my seat to quietly read the story and answer the ten questions in my notebook in complete sentences. When complete, I would bring my notebook up to the teacher's desk to be marked. The teacher marked the answers. If I had answered the questions correctly, she stamped my book loudly and announced to the class the color I was moving on to: "Adrienne Gear has just moved up to MUSTARD #3!" Everyone would stop working and watch as I walked proudly back to the SRA kit and changed my card. Then I sat back in my desk to begin the process again. If you went up to the teacher's desk and did not get a stamp and announcement, the silence echoed as you returned to your desk to do the dreaded corrections.

Most of the questions on the SRA cards were literal questions. I discovered rather early in this process—as many children do—that I, in fact, did not actually have to read the story in order to be able to answer most of the questions. I just found the answer right in the text, turned the question into a statement answer and moved on to the next question. But the questions usually saved for the end were not literal. They were the "What if… ?" "Why…?" "Why do you think…?" questions. Those answers, no matter how hard I looked, were not anywhere to be found on the card. I consistently struggled with those questions, not only because I hadn't actually read the story but, I now realize, because nobody showed me how to answer them. I was never taught that answers that are not right there in the text need to come from me. These are the questions that take us deeper into the story and really demonstrate whether understanding has taken place. But I wanted the right answer, and I was not confident enough to rely on my own thinking to find the answers to those questions within myself. It goes without saying that I spent my Grade 7 year "stuck in the Mustard." I never made it up to those coveted Goldenrod cards, no matter how much I longed to hear my teacher's loud stamp on my notebook.

As with so much of the Reading Power program, the strategy of Questioning is deeply rooted in the memory of my experience in that Grade 7 class. My struggle with inferential questions stemmed from a lack of modeling and instruction. Therefore, I want to ensure that students are supported—not only in being able to answer questions that require thinking beyond the surface of the story, but in their ability to ask them as well.

Certainly, when I first began teaching, I was like my Grade 7 teacher, an assign-and-assess instructor: "Read this and answer these questions." I loved a teacher's guide with all the answers provided because it made the assessing part quick and easy. The *Answers Will Vary* questions were less convenient, because they meant I really had to read the child's answer carefully. But now I realize that, if we are to help our students become confident strategic thinkers and learners, it is imperative that the questions we ask encourage them to go beyond the literal surface of the story to a place where thinking is nurtured. So, too, do we need to encourage them to wonder while they read. Answering comprehension questions at the end of a chapter does not encourage wonderment and deep thinking; teaching students to ask questions that reach beyond the surface of the story does.

> "The answers aren't important really. What's important is knowing all the questions."
> — Z.K. Snyder, *The Changeling*

> "No one questions, wonders, no one examines like children. It is not simply that children love questions, but that they live questions."
> —Christopher Phillips, *The Philosopher's Club*

When readers learn to question while reading:

- they are learning the power of asking as well as answering questions.
- they are encouraged to be curious readers.
- they learn that asking questions can lead them to a greater understanding of the text.
- they learn the difference between quick questions and deep-thinking questions.
- they learn that not all questions have answers, and often these unanswered questions will help to get at the heart of the story better than those that can be answered.
- they practise what their Power-ful brains are already capable of doing—asking questions.

Introducing the Power to Question

Prior to working through some lessons to model the Question strategy, I spend time immersing students in the notion of questions. Interestingly enough, when asked what "question words" they know, most students come up with the classic *Who? What? Where? When? Why?* It is interesting to have the class brainstorm other question words, and then to leave these up in the classroom for reference (see Questioning Words chart on page 61).

It is also important to introduce students to the two types of questions that good readers (and good thinkers) ask while they read. There are many different terms for these two types of questions: literal and inferential; thick and thin (Harvey & Goudvis, pp. 89, 90); right-there and in-your-head. I have termed them *quick questions* and *deep-thinking questions* (see Questioning Words chart on page 61). Whichever term you choose to use, I believe children need to be introduced to the idea: Good readers ask questions while they read; some answers can be found right in the story, but if you can't find the answer in the story, the answer has to come from you. Again, it is this reinforcement of metacognition—awareness of thinking, of understanding, of questioning and answering—that empowers students to become more confident constructors of meaning. Awareness leads to understanding.

Sequential Lessons for Questioning

Lesson 1 (Teacher Directed): Introducing the Power

- Using the Reading Powers Model, add the Question puzzle piece to the child's head.
- Explain that good readers ask questions before they read, while they read, and after they read (see Three Stages of Questioning #1 and #2 on pages 59, 60).
- Choose one or two books to help illustrate the notion of Deep Thinking Questions to read aloud to the class: *I Wonder Why* by Lois Rock or *I Wonder* by Tana Hoban (Primary); *The Philosopher's Club* by Christopher Phillips or *The Day Eddie Met the Author* by Louise Borden (Intermediate).
- Brainstorm a list of question words beyond the "5 W's" on chart paper that you can keep up in your classroom.

"Quick questions are questions that have answers you can find right in the book. Deep-thinking questions are questions that, no matter how hard you look in the story, you will never find the answer right there. If the answer is not in the story, the answer needs to come from your thinking."

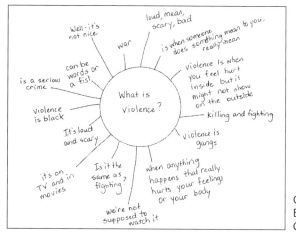

Grades 6/7 Class Responses
Book: *The Philosopher's Club* by Christopher Phillips

Lessons 2–4 (Teacher Directed/ Independent Work): Extending Deep-Thinking Questions

- Spend one or two lessons working on practising, discussing, and asking deep-thinking questions.
- Students illustrate their own deep-thinking questions; make a class book.
- After reading *If* by Sarah Perry, have students choose one of the "What if's" from the book. Using the IF… Web on page 62, have them write six different questions stemming from it.
- Using the same web, students create their own "What if" inside the web. They write a question in one of the bubbles and pass the web to another student. The second student reads the "what if" and the question, then adds a question and passes it along. This continues until the web is complete.
- Choose one of the questions from book *The Philosopher's Club* by Christopher Phillips and write it in the centre of a web (see IF… Web on page 62) copied onto large chart paper. (Examples: *What is violence? What is silence? Is it possible to be happy and sad at the same time?*) Discuss the question with your students and model how you might add a response, a reaction, or another question to the web. Over the next few days, invite the students to add their own responses to the question. When the web is full, read and share the responses. Compliment your students on their deep thinking.

Grade 5 Sample
Book: *If* by Sarah Perry

Lessons 5–6 (Teacher Directed): Group Questioning

- Model and read-aloud/think-aloud a book from the Gem bag. Ask questions aloud as you read, marking your questions with sticky notes (as you did in the first few Connect lessons).
- Afterwards, peel off the notes and stick them to one side of a chart paper that is divided into columns: Answered in the Text?; Does It Matter? (see Evaluating Questions #1 on page 63).
- Go through each question and check off the appropriate column on the chart. Discuss the fact that those questions that did not get answered (deep-thinking questions) are often the ones that encourage us to think.

The "Does It Matter?" column evolved from a group lesson I was teaching with a Grade 6 class. One student kept writing completely irrelevant questions about *Mr. Bear and the Bear* by Frances Thomas: "How many hairs are on the bear's head? How much was the mortgage on the old man's house?" He then claimed that they must be deep-thinking questions, because none had been answered in the text. Answers to deep-thinking questions may not be found in the story, but they certainly need to matter.

- Divide the class into groups and give each group a deep-thinking question from the book. Have the students discuss the answers. This could be done as a "carousel" activity: a different deep-thinking question from the story is written on the top of one of several chart papers. Groups of students rotate to each question, recording their answers on the chart paper.
- Repeat lesson next day using a different book.
- Suggested books for this lesson: *The Wednesday Surprise* and *Charlie Anderson* by Eve Bunting, *Sami and the Time of the Troubles* by Florence Parry Heide, and *The Jupiter Stone* by Paul Owen Lewis.

Lessons 7–8 (Guided Practice): Your Turn to Question

- Choose a story from the Gem list.
- Give each student three or four sticky notes. Explain to the students that while you are reading you would like them to "pay attention to their thinking" while they read. Each time they wonder something about the story, they can write the question on one of the stickies and come up to stick it in the book. For younger students, scribe the students' questions on the sticky notes yourself (I usually set a limit or one or two questions per page if I'm scribing questions for primary students).
- Hold up the book, read the title, and ask "What are you wondering about this book?" All students should use their first sticky to ask a question from the cover and title.
- Continue reading, stopping after each page and asking, "Now what are you wondering about?" Students may run out of stickies, but they can continue to wonder in their heads.

The questions can also be recorded on one of the Three Stages of Questioning forms on pages 59 and 60.

- After the story is complete, remove the sticky notes and stick them onto a chart paper with the columns labeled as in Evaluating Questions #1 on page 63. Repeated questions can be stuck on top of each other. Proceed through the same routine as in Lessons 5–6, checking off whether the questions were answered in the story or not.
- Students discuss answers to one or two deep-thinking questions (in pairs or small groups).
- Suggested books for this lesson: *Mr. Bear and the Bear* by Frances Thomas, *The Cinder-Eyed Cats* by Eric Rohmann, *Frog Belly Rat Bone* by Timothy Basil Ering, and *The Summer My Father Was Ten* by Pat Bisson.

Providing opportunities for students to answer deep-thinking questions is laying the groundwork for their later experience with the power to infer answers to deep-thinking questions.

Lessons 9–10 (Independent Practice): Choose Your Own Question Book

- Students choose their own books from the Question Bin and, while they read, record their questions on sticky notes or one of the Three Stages of Questioning forms (pages 63 and 64).
- Have students remove the sticky notes with questions and place them in order down the left side of Evaluating Questions #1 on page 63, or use Evaluating Questions #2 on page 64. They check off whether each of the questions was answered in the story or not.
- Have students choose one of the questions that was not answered in the text and answer this question on the bottom of the page.

Lesson 11–12 (Independent Practice): Asking and Answering Questions

- Repeat steps in previous lesson, but this time, rather than simply checking whether or not the questions were answered, have the students answer their questions in sentences.
- Remind the students the difference between answering a quick question and a deep-thinking question: if the answer was found in the story, their answer needs to be written in the form of a statement; e.g., Q: What was the boy's name? A: The boy's name was Zac. If the answer was not found directly in the book, the answer will need to begin with "I think" or "Maybe."

Reading Power

Questioning

Title: The sand children   Author: Joyce Dunbar

Questions we had while we read	Answered	
	Yes	No
I wonder if the sandboy will come alive?	✓	
Why are they camping on the beach?		✓
Why did he build a sand giant?		✓
Wouldn't they go back home?		✓
Do they live there?		✓
Why are there Dancing?		✓
Why does he need to do the faces?		✓
If he wouldn't wake up then who will do the tapes?	✓	
Was it a dream?		✓

Grade 3 Sample

Mr Bear and the Bear
by Frances Thomas

1 Why is Mr Bear so grumpy?
D-T
I think Mr Bear is grumpy because he is very lonley and he maybe because he doesn't have any friends or relatives.

2. Why is the man making the bear dance?
Q-Q
The man is making the bear because he wants every one to think that he is so great that he trained a bear that can dance.

3 What is Mr Bear going to do with the Bear?
S-W
I think Mr Bear is going to keep the bear as a pet.

4 Is the bear going to stay with Mr Bear?
D-T
I think the bear is going to stay with Mr Bear.

Grade 4 Sample

Lesson 13: Reflective Journal

Have students record their thoughts about this new reading power in their journals. "How does asking questions while you read help you understand the story better? Show me or tell me about your thinking."

> asking questions helps me to understand the story better because asking questions makes us curiouse and being curiouse makes us wont to find out the answers and plns it makes us wonder; ✓

Question Booklist

Gems for Modeling Think-Alouds and Guided Practice

P = primary
I = intermediate
SR = social responsibility
A = Aboriginal

If we want our students to understand what questioning is, we need to show them what it looks like. It is important to spend time modeling your own think-aloud questions. Here are some books for teachers to use in these modeling lessons

REALISTIC STORIES

Abercrombie, Barbara. *Charlie Anderson.* (P, I)
Bisson, Pat. *The Summer My Father Was Ten.* (SR) (I)
Borden, Louise. *The Day Eddie Met the Author.* (I)
Bunting, Eve. *Fly Away Home.* (I)
Elvgren, Jennifer Riesmeyer. *Josias, Hold the Book.* (I)
Garland, Sherry. *The Lotus Seed.* (I)
Harris, Dorothy Joan. *A Very Unusual Dog.* (P)
Hoban, Tana. *I Wonder.* (P)
Heide, Florence. *The Day of Ahmed's Secret.* (I)
Irving, John. *A Sound Like Someone Trying Not to Make a Sound.* (P, I)
Koss, Amy Goldman. *Where Fish Go in Winter.* (P, I)
Phillips, Christopher. *The Philosopher's Club.* (I)
Rock, Lois. *I Wonder Why.* (P, I)
Thomas, Frances. *Mr. Bear and the Bear.* (P, I)
Wallace, Ian. *Boy of the Deeps.* (I)

FANTASY STORIES

Berger, Barbara. *Grandfather Twilight.* (P)
Browne, Anthony. *Changes.* (P, I)
Ering, Timothy Basil. *The Story of Frog Belly Rat Bone.* (P, I)
Kitamura, Satoshi. *UFO Diary.* (I)
Lewis, Paul Owen. *The Jupiter Stone.* (I)
Lewis, Paul Owen. *Storm Boy.* (I) (A)
Merriam, Eve. *The Wise Woman and Her Secret.* (P, I)
Perry, Sarah. *If.* (P, I)
Robertson, M.P. *The Egg.* (P, I)
Robertson, M.P. *The Sandcastle.* (P, I)
Rohmann, Eric. *The Cinder-Eyed Cats.* (P, I)
Rohmann, Eric. *Time Flies.* (P, I)
Rosenberg, Liz. *The Carousel.* (P, I)
Say, Allan. *Stranger in the Mirror.* (I)
Scheer, Julian. *By the Light of the Captured Moon.* (I)
Sendak, Maurice. *Where the Wild Things Are.* (P)

P = primary
I = intermediate
SR = social responsibility
A = Aboriginal

Once the students are ready to practise questioning independently, they can choose books from the Question bin. Choose from the following books to create a collection of Question books for your classroom.

REALISTIC STORIES

Alderson, Sue Ann. *Ida and the Wool Smugglers.* (P, I)

Best, Cari. *Goose's Story.* (P, I)

Bunting, Eve. *Gleam and Glow.* (I)

Bunting, Eve. *The Wednesday Surprise.* (P, I)

Carmen, William. *What's That Noise?* (P)

Chinn, Karen. *Sam and the Lucky Money.* (SR) (P, I)

Christiansen, Candace. *The Mitten Tree.* (P, I)

Coerr, Eleanor. *Sadako.* (I)

Cumming, Peter. *Out on the Ice in the Middle of the Bay.* (P, I) (A)

Dabcovich, Lydia. *The Polar Bear Son.* (P, I) (A)

Erdrich, Louise. *Grandmother's Pigeon.* (I)

Gilliland, Judith Heide. *Not in the House, Newton!* (P, I)

Hathorn, Libby. *Way Home.* (SR) (I)

Heide, Florence. *The Day of Ahmed's Secret.* (P, I)

Heide, Florence Parry. *Sami and the Time of the Troubles.* (P, I)

Khan, Rukhsana. *King of the Skies.* (I)

Khan, Rukhsana. *The Roses in My Carpet.* (I)

Lasky, Kathryn. *The Librarian Who Measured the Earth.* (I)

McGovern, Ann. *The Lady in the Box.* (SR) (P, I)

Martin, Rafe. *The Boy Who Lived with the Seals.* (P, I) (A)

Martin, Rafe. *Rough-Faced Girl.* (P, I) (A)

Nikly, Michelle. *The Perfume of Memory.* (I)

Schuch, Steve. *A Symphony of Whales.* (I)

Spalding, Andrea. *Me and Mr. Mah.* (I)

Spalding, Andrea. *Solomon's Tree.* (P, I) (A)

Trottier, Maxine. *Claire's Gift.* (P, I)

Trottier, Maxine. *Dreamstones.* (I)

Trottier, Maxine. *Flags.* (P, I)

Trottier, Maxine. *The Tiny Kite of Eddie Wing.* (I)

Vaage, Carol. *Bibi and the Bull.* (P)

Whetung, James. *The Vision Seeker.* (I) (A)

Williams, Vera B. *A Chair for My Mother.* (P, I)

FANTASY STORIES

Demers, Dominique. *Old Thomas and the Little Fairy.* (P, I)

Dunbar, Joyce. *The Sand Children.* (P, I)

Feiffer, Jules. *Meanwhile.* (P, I)

Fleischman, Paul. *Weslandia.* (I)

Gay, Marie-Louise. *Mademoiselle Moon.* (P, I)

Gay, Marie-Louise. *Stella, Fairy of the Forest.* (P, I)

Gay, Marie-Louise. *Stella, Star of the Sea.* (P, I)

Gay, Marie-Louise. *Stella, Queen of the Snow.* (P, I)

Harrison, Troon. *The Dream Collector.* (P, I)

Haseley, Dennis. *A Story For Bear.* (I)

Johnston, Karen. *Mr. Bob's Magic Ride in the Sky.* (I)

Joyce, William. *A Day With Wilbur Johnson.* (P, I)

Lee, Lyn. *Pog.* (P)

Lewis, Paul Owen. *Frog Girl.* (I)

McAllistar, Andrew. *Snow Angel.* (P, I)

McElligott, Matthew. *Uncle Frank's Pit.* (P, I)

Nelson, S.D. *The Star People: A Lakota Story.* (P, I) (A)

Nolan, Dennis. *Dinosaur Dreams.* (P, I)

Oram, Hiawyn. *In the Attic.* (P, I)

Rohmann, Eric. *Clara and Asha.* (P)

Rylant, Cynthia. *The Van Gogh Café.* (I)

Steig, William. *Brave Irene.* (P, I)

Steig, William. *Doctor De Soto.* (P, I)

Steig, William. *Spinky Sulks.* (P, I)

Steig, William. *Sylvester and the Magic Pebble.* (P, I)

Swope, Sam. *The Araboolies of Liberty Street.* (I)

Tavares, Matt. *Zachary's Ball.* (P, I)

Teague, Mark. *Lost and Found.* (P, I)

Teague, Mark. *The Secret Shortcut.* (P, I)

Turkle, Brinton. *Do Not Open.* (P,)

Wargin, Kathy-Jo. *The Legend of the Loon.* (I)

Wood, Audrey. *The Flying Dragon Room.* (P, I)

Wynn Jones, Tim. *Architect of the Moon.* (P)

Three Stages of Questioning #1

Name: _____ Date: _____

Title: _____ Author: _____

These are some questions I had **before** I started reading:

_____

_____

_____

_____

These are some questions I had **while** I was reading:

_____

_____

_____

_____

These are some questions I had **after** I finished reading this book:

_____

_____

_____

_____

Three Stages of Questioning #2

Name: _____   Date: _____

Title: _____   Author: _____

Questions I have…

Before reading

During reading

After reading

Questioning Words

When we read, we can ask…

Quick Questions	Deep-Thinking Questions
• quick to ask • quick to answer • answer is right there in the book (literal thinking)	• answer is not in the book • answer comes from you ("I think…", "Maybe…") (inferential thinking) • often there is no one right answer • usually lead to more questions • help us think beyond the story • need *to matter*

Question Words	
who	what
where	when
why	how
would	wouldn't
what if	what about
do	don't
does	doesn't
is	isn't
did	didn't
could	couldn't
can	can't
are	aren't
should	shouldn't
I wonder	

IF... Web

Name: _____

Date: _____

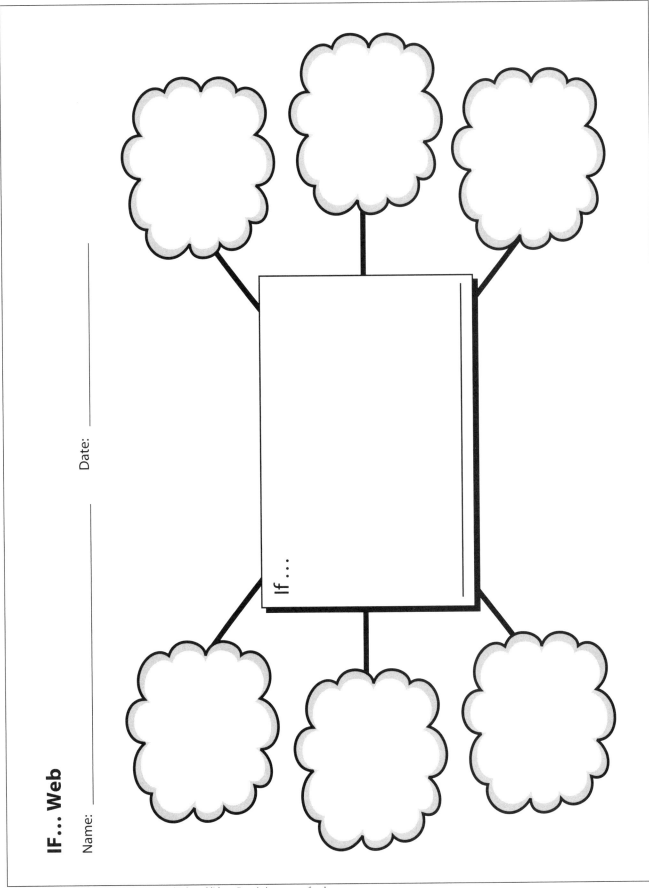

If . . .

Evaluating Questions #1

Name: _____   Date: _____

Title: _____   Author: _____

Questions we had while we read	Answered in Text		Does it Matter?	
	Yes	No	Yes	No

Choose one of the questions that was not answered in the story but that matters to the story and write what you think.

Question: _____

Answer: I think… _____

Evaluating Questions #2

Name: _____   Date: _____

Title: _____   Author: _____

Questions I had while I read	A	NA	BK	NR	SW

A   =   answered
NA =   not answered
BK =   background knowledge
NR =   needs research
SW =   still wondering

5   The Power to Visualize

Visualize Chant

(snap or clap the beat)

You don't use your eyes when you visualize
You don't use your eyes when you visualize
You don't use your eyes when you visualize
You use your brain! Yah!

Visualize Song

(to the tune of "Twinkle, Twinkle, Little Star")

When my teacher reads a book
Then my brain begins to look!
Seeing pictures in my head
As the story's being read,
Making pictures, me and you.
You can THINK some pictures too!

(Diane Martin, Spul'u'kwuks School)

✳ ✳ ✳

"When your head is full of pictures, they just have to come out."
—Bill Maynard, *Incredible Ned*

During a long car ride, an eight-year-old boy passes the time listening to a tape recording of *The Hatchet* by Gary Paulson. For nearly three hours, he does not speak and is completely absorbed in the story. Later that night, when his mother is tucking him in, he comments, "That was the best movie I've ever seen."

"What movie?" asks his mother.

"That one in the car," he replies.

"But that wasn't a movie," explains his mother, "that was a tape recording."

"Really?" responds the boy. "But I saw the whole thing in my head!" This boy has demonstrated the amazing ability of the mind's eye to create images from text—the power to visualize.

Visualizing and connecting are very closely related. These, above all other strategies, call upon the reader to draw from their own experiences to help make sense of the text. Whether making a connection or making a picture in one's mind, the source from which one connects or creates images is one's well of experiences, one's memory bank. Visualizing is the sister to imagination; one could argue that they are one and the same. The source from which the images are created is the only difference. When we use our imaginations, the source for the images created comes from within; when we visualize, the source for the images created comes from the text.

Visualizing is not difficult to do. I believe all children have the ability to close their eyes and imagine or make pictures in their heads. Unfortunately, with the amount of TV viewing in many of our students' homes, the visualizing function in the brain may be in need of some exercise. The problem may also arise, as it does when teaching and practising connecting, with some readers' lack of experiences; e.g., it is difficult to visualize a beach when one has never been to the beach. When teaching and practising visualizing with children, it is important to choose books that describe things that your students will be familiar with, so that the images they create come easily. ESL students may require some pre-reading language or vocabulary building so that they have a fuller portfolio of images on which to draw when they begin to visualize. Most of the books used when teaching and practising this strategy are very descriptive, filled with rich, descriptive, and poetic language that helps the reader create mental images easily. Books that describe weather, seasons, or specific places or things tend to work best.

When readers learn to visualize while reading:

- they are using the words they hear or read in a text to create visual images or "movies in the mind" (Harvey & Goudvis, p. 11).
- they can turn on their brains just as they would turn on their TVs, to enjoy the many images they can create.
- they are training their brains for when they begin to read books that don't include pictures with the text.
- they are encouraged to activate their imaginations as they read.
- they combine their own background knowledge with the words of the author to create mental images that enhance understanding of the text and bring reading to life.
- they are able to activate all their senses to create mental images.
- it is most likely when reading books about places, weather, or seasons that are filled with rich, descriptive, and vivid language.

Introducing the Power to Visualize

To begin students visualizing, I take them through a series of quick visualizing exercises, followed by a longer activity. These lessons illustrate four important points:

1. Visualizing is relatively simple to do.
2. "Picture words" help readers visualize.
3. The pictures we make in our heads are created from our own experiences.
4. Visualizing involves not only things we see, but also our other senses.

Quick Visualizing Exercises

- Tell the students that you are going to say a word, and ask them to make a picture in their heads of that word. Start out with a simple noun such as "rainbow."
- Give the students a few seconds to visualize, then ask them who had a picture of a rainbow in their heads. Most students are able to do this without too much difficulty.
- Move on to other terms; e.g., "ice cream cone," "pencil crayons," "dog." After each, have students pair up and share their images: *What flavor was your ice cream? What kind of dog did you visualize?*
- Then, complicate the exercise by using a word that does not evoke a simple image; e.g., "the," "do," "at."
- After a few of these words, ask the students which words were easier to visualize. Explain to the students that not all words help readers visualize, but certain words, called "picture words," will really help them to make their pictures clearly. It is important for readers to pay attention to picture words to help them visualize.

Visualizing Activity

I introduce the activity the same way for all students:

Younger students will tend to "act out" the story as it is told, so it is important to stress to them that when we visualize, the only part of the body that is moving is our brains.

> I'm going to tell you a story and, while I'm telling the story, I'd like you to close your eyes and visualize. See if you can make a picture or a movie in your mind while you listen to the story. Then we're going to talk about the pictures you made. Everybody, close your eyes and remember that when you are visualizing, the only part of your body that should be moving is your brain. Here we go…

Use this "story" for Primary students to visualize.

> I want you to visualize a lollipop. This lollipop is on a white stick and it has a wrapper on it. Visualize yourself holding this lollipop. I want you to notice the color and shape and size of this lollipop. Some lollipops are big, and some are small, some are round and some are flat —what does yours look like? Now I want you to visualize yourself taking off the wrapper. Listen to the sound as you take the wrapper off. Put the wrapper in the garbage. Now I would like you to visualize yourself taking a lick of the lollipop. What flavor is your lollipop? Take another lick. Now put the lollipop, if it's not too big, in your mouth. Suck on it for a while. Listen to the sound it makes when it hits your teeth. Now take a bite. Listen to the sound the bite makes. Now crunch your lollipop and really get the flavor in your mouth. Some of the candy sticks in your teeth. Now visualize yourself as you take the lollipop out of your mouth. Look at what is left on your stick. Open your eyes.

For Intermediate students, the school setting and element of mystery require more complex visualizing.

> It is recess time at your school. I want you to visualize yourself outside somewhere on the school playground or school grounds. Where are you? Take a moment to look around you. What can you see from where you are standing? What sounds can you hear? What is the weather like? Visualize yourself eating a recess snack. Take a bite. What are you tasting right now? Keep eating your snack. Suddenly you hear someone calling your name. Visualize yourself looking around to try to locate where the sound is coming from. You suddenly see someone you know very well running towards you. The person is calling your name and has something in his or her hands. This person reaches you, talking very quickly and seeming very excited to show you what is in his or her hands. The person shows you and tells you about it. You ask if you can hold it. Visualize yourself holding the object. Now someone else comes to join you and you all look at this thing. Suddenly, the bell rings. Visualize yourself running with your friends to the nearest door and walk towards your classroom. Open your eyes.

Ask the following questions:

- Who had a movie in their heads while I told that story?
- Who had a colored movie? Whose movie was black and white?
- Who had sounds in their movie? Tastes? Feelings?

Point out to the students that "visualizing" is not just about things we see. When we visualize, we are actually using all five senses: sights, sounds, tastes, touch, and smells.

Write the following questions on a chart stand. Have the students find partners to share the following information:

Primary	Intermediate
1. What color was your lollipop?	1. Where were you on the playground?
2. What size?	2. What was the weather like?
3. What shape?	3. What was your recess snack?
4. What flavor?	4. What sounds could you hear?
5. After you took a bite, what did your lollipop look like?	5. Who was calling your name?
	6. What object did the person show you?

After this sharing time, continue:

Raise your hand if you and your partner had exactly the same size, shape, color, and flavor of lollipop? (same place, snack, person, and object?)

(Occasionally, partners have similar answers,
but generally speaking the "mind movies" are all different
because the students naturally visualized
from their own experiences.)

Well, that is very interesting. But how could it be that everyone in the room heard the same story but visualized different things? How can that be possible?"

This exercise illustrates very clearly the same point that is made when introducing connecting: because we are all different, with different experiences and different memories, each person's visualizing is going to be different. Just as we make connections from our own experiences, we visualize from what we know.

Sequential Lessons for Visualizing

Lesson 1 (Teacher Directed): Introducing the Power

- Explain to the class what visualizing is—making a picture in your head when you read. Explain that when they begin reading chapter books, there are no pictures, so they have to practise making pictures in their heads.
- Go through a few single-image visualizing exercises. Have students listen practise quick visualizing of single words. Introduce the concept of picture words (see page 66).
- Have students practise visualizing by closing their and trying to "make a movie" in their heads while you tell a story. Remind students that, like when they are making connections, everyone makes slightly different pictures in their heads because everyone is different. (See pages 67–68 for script and questions.)

"When there are no pictures in the book, you have to make pictures in your head."

"Artists use colors to paint pictures; authors use words to help their readers paint pictures in their heads."

Lesson 2 (Teacher Directed): Modeling Visualizing on Paper

Cover the books used for modeling the Visualize strategy with paper so students cannot see any illustrations.

- To model the strategy, ask another teacher (or librarian, non-enrolling teacher, administrator) to come into your class to help. You will be reading aloud a Gem from the Visualizing Book Bin. Cover the book with paper so that nobody can see the pictures or the title. Divide the book into four sections.
- Make and number four large squares on chart paper.
- Begin to read the first section of the book slowly. The teacher who is modeling begins to make quick sketches in box #1 while you read. Students are visualizing at the same time.
- When the teacher finishes the sketch, ask him or her to write one or two "picture words" that really helped them visualize.
- Invite the teacher to turn the chart stand around and do a point-and-talk with the picture. Respond to the teacher's drawings with comments: "I like the way you just drew a stick person rather than too many details" "I like the way you filled the whole box with images."
- Repeat this process with the three remaining sections of the story, having the teacher draw in different boxes each time, record picture words, and do a point-and-talk.
- After the story is finished, have students and other teacher predict the title.

I usually turn the chart stand around so that the children are not all staring at the teacher while she or he draws.

- Finally, reveal the cover and title and read the book again, showing the pictures.
- Suggested books for this lesson: *Splish, Splash, Spring* by Jan Carr, *Puddles* by Jonathan London.

Lesson 3 (Guided Group Practice): Visualizing on Paper Together

- Repeat Lesson 1: using chart paper divided into four, have four different students come up to draw in each box. The other students can visualize in their heads while you read.
- After each student draws, ask them to record one or two picture words and share their pictures with the class by doing a point-and-talk.
- Suggested books for this lesson: *Garden* by Jesse Ostrow (very simple text); *Rain, Drop, Splash* by Alvin Tresselt; *Seasons* by John Burningham; *A Windy Day* by Halina Below; and *In the Small, Small Pond* by Denise Fleming.

Samples from Grade 1 and Grade 4
Book: *The Seashore Book* by Charlotte Zolotow

We want students to do quick sketches. Too many colors can be distracting. I usually have them choose only one color or use a pencil.

Although most of the visualizing sketches do not involve coloring, I allow students time to color their pictures in this lesson.

Lessons 4–5 (Independent Practice): Visualizing on Paper on Your Own

- Give students the Visualizing sheet on page 75 or divide a paper into four.
- Read aloud the book (no cover or pictures showing) and ask students to make quick drawings in box #1 while you read the first part of the book. After you finish, ask them to write one or two picture words that helped them visualize that part of the story.
- Have the students do a point-and-talk with a partner about their first box.
- Continue reading the story, stopping after each section to do a point-and-talk with a partner.
- At the end of the story, ask the students to write what they think the title of the book is. Have some students share their ideas with the class
- Reveal the cover and title, and read the story again to the class, this time showing the pictures.

Lesson 6 (Independent Practice): Single-Image Visualizing

- Repeat Lessons 4–5 Visualizing on Paper on Your Own, having students draw one large image instead of four small ones. Provide large pieces of white paper for the students to create a single image.
- You may need to read the text several times over to allow students to add details to their sketches.
- Have students share their pictures with a partner, and then allow time to go back to their own pictures to add details.
- Have students write their prediction of the title of the book on their pictures. Read the title, and show the students the illustrations from the book.
- Suggested books for this lesson: *My Garden* by Jesse Ostrow (works well for K–1); *The Seashore Book* by Charlotte Zolotow; *Oh Canada* (photo images to the words of the national anthem) published by Scholastic; *In the Small, Small Pond* by Denise Flemming; *The Forest* (Queen Charlotte Island Reader); and *Where the Forest Meets the Sea* by Jeannie Baker.

Grade 1 Sample
Book: *My Garden* by Jesse Ostrow

Lessons 7–8 (Guided Practice): Introducing Using Your Senses

- Introduce students to the Using Our Senses grid on page 76. Explain that when we read, we not only can see pictures in our heads, but we can also use our other senses to hear sounds, taste tastes, feel objects.
- Reproduce the Using Our Senses grid on chart paper. Read aloud and have students come up and write (or draw) in the boxes when they hear, see, smell, feel, or taste things.

- Suggested books for this lesson: *Gilberto and the Wind* by Marie Hall Ets, *In November* by Cynthia Rylant, *Wild Child* by Lynn Plourde, *Hello Ocean* by Pam Munoz Ryan, *Owl Moon* by Jane Yolen, *Night Sounds, Morning Colors* by Rosemary Wells.

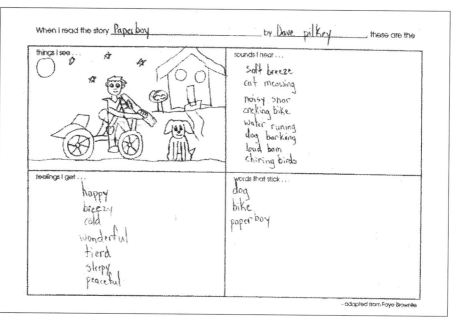

Grade 4 Sample

Lesson 9 (Independent Practice): Using Your Senses to Visualize

Repeat the previous group lesson, but choose a new book and have students work on their own papers while you read aloud.

Lessons 10–11 (Guided/Independent Practice): Visualizing a Character

- Find a detailed description of a character from a book. Character descriptions from novels work well for this lesson: e.g., description of Willy Wonka from *Charlie and the Chocolate Factory* by Roald Dahl (pp. 60–61).
- Without telling students the name of the book or character, have them visualize the character, then draw and color a detailed picture of the character.
- When everyone is finished, have the students display their pictures. Ask "Why do you think everyone's picture is so similar?" Point out that good writers use such specific picture words when they write, it helps the reader visualize very clearly.
- Have students create their own character and draw it in as much detail as possible. On a separate piece of paper, have them write a description of the created character, including as many picture words as they can think of about size, height, hair/eye/skin color, interesting features, clothes, special objects, etc.
- Collect the completed written descriptions and pass them out randomly.
- Students read the description that another student has written and try to draw a picture of that character. Illustrators then pair up with authors to compare drawings and see how accurately the pictures match their descriptions.

Lesson 12 (Guided/Independent Practice): Draw and Reflect
(adapted from Debbie Miller)

- Choose any book from the Visualizing Book Bin. Read aloud the entire book without showing students the cover or illustrations.

To keep students from copying pictures from the book when drawing their images, I ask them to put the book back. Then I say, "You are a magical photographer who can step inside the book to take pictures, but you can take just four pictures. Which four pictures stick in your mind?"

- Ask students to choose one picture they visualized during the story that really stuck in their minds. Using one of the Visualize, Draw, and Reflect grids on pages 77 and 78, have students draw their images and then write about their choice.
- This lesson can be repeated with students choosing their own books. To avoid copying, have students have students read through the book a couple of times and then put it back into the Book Bin. Then have them draw an image from memory.
- Suggested books for this lesson: *What a Wonderful World* by George David Weiss, *Baby Beluga* by Raffi.

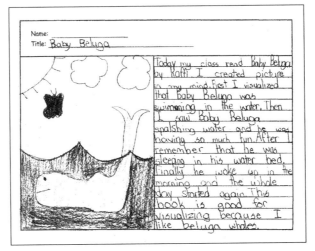

Lesson 13: Reflective Journal

Have students record their thoughts about this new strategy and what they've learned about visualizing. "How has visualizing while you read helped you to understand the story better? Show me or tell me about your thinking."

Other Visualize Lessons

- Students use the Visualizing During Reading chart on page 79, or the Listening for Picture Words template on page 80 while reading their own Visualize book.
- Students choose a passage in a novel they are reading and create an illustration for it.
- Students visualize their own special place (e.g., a room, a park, their bedroom, a tent, the view from a window) and write a descriptive passage about it.

Visualize Booklist

P = primary
I = intermediate
SR = social responsibility
A = Aboriginal

Gems for Modeling Think-Alouds and Guided Practice

If we want our students to understand what visualizing is, we need to show them what it looks like. It is important to spend time modeling your own think-aloud visualizations. Here are some books for teachers to use in these modeling lessons.

DESCRIPTIVE (PLACE, PERSONAL)

Alborough, Jez. *Watch Out, Big Bro Is Coming!* (P)
Baker, Keith. *Little Green.* (P)
Baker, Keith. *Who Is the Beast?* (P, I)
Brown, Margaret Wise. *The Big Red Barn.* (P)
Carroll, Lewis. *Jabberwocky.* (P, I)
Demers, Dominique. *Every Single Night.* (P, I)
Duksta, Laura. *I Love You More.* (P)
Fleming, Denise. *In the Small, Small Pond.* (P)
Hamanaka, Sheila. *All the Colors of the Earth.* (P, I)
Heidbreder, Robert. *I Wished for a Unicorn.* (P, I)
Henderson, Kathy. *The Little Boat.* (P)
Highway, Tomson. *Fox on the Ice.* (P, I) (A)
Lawson, Julie. *Kate's Castle.* (I)
Liao, Jimmy. *The Sound of Colors.* (I)
Ostrow, Jesse. *My Garden.* (P)
Ryder, Joanne. *Chipmunk Song.* (P, I)
Ryder, Joanne. *The Waterfall's Gift.* (I)
St. Pierre, Stephanie. *What the Sea Saw.* (P, I)
Thong, Roseanne. *Round Is a Mooncake.* (P)

Weiss, George David. *What a Wonderful World.* (P)
Wells, Rosemary. *Night Sounds, Morning Colors.* (P, I)
Yolen, Jane. *Owl Moon.* (P, I)
Zolotow, Charlotte. *The Seashore Book.* (P, I)

SEASONAL

Burningham, John. *Seasons.* (P)
Carr, Jan. *Splish, Splash, Spring!* (P)
Chase, Newlin. *Waters.* (P)
Gerber, Mary J. *Thanks for Thanksgiving.* (P)
Plourde, Lynn. *Wild Child.* (P, I)
Rylant, Cynthia. *In November.* (I)

WEATHER

Below, Halina. *The Windy Day.* (P, I)
Ets, Marie Hall. *Gilberto and the Wind.* (P)
Fitch, Sheree. *No Two Snowflakes.* (P, I)
Keats, Ezra Jack. *The Snowy Day.* (P)
London, Jonathon. *Puddles.* (P, I)
Ray, May Lyn. *Mud.* (P, I)
Tresselt, Alvin. *Rain, Drop, Splash.* (P)

Books for Independent Practice

P = primary
I = intermediate
SR = social responsibility
A = Aboriginal

Once the students are ready to practise visualizing independently, they can choose books from the Visualizing bin. Choose from the following books to create a collection of Visualizing books for your classroom

DESCRIPTIVE (PLACE, PERSONAL)

Adams, Dawn. *The Forest.* (P)
Baker, Jeannie. *Where the Forest Meets the Sea.* (P, I)
Baylor, Bird. *Guess Who My Favorite Person Is.* (I)
Bogart, Jo Ellen. *The Night the Stars Flew.* (P)
Brown, Margaret Wise. *Sailor Dog.* (P)
Bunting, Eve. *The Sunflower House.* (P, I)
Chase, Edith Newlin. *Secret Dawn.* (P, I)
Coy, John. *Night Driving.* (I)
Crum, Shutta. *Click!* (P)
Dahl, Roald. *Charlie and the Chocolate Factory.* (I)

Dene Children of La Loche and Friends. *Byron Through the Seasons: A Dene-English Story Book. (Byron Bel Haet'aziluke sine.)* (P, I) (A)
Edwards, Pamela Duncan. *Some Smug Slug.* (P)
Fleischman, Paul. *The Sidewalk Circus.* (I)
Fleming, Denise. *In the Tall, Tall Grass.* (P)
Harter, Debbie. *Walking Through the Jungle.* (P)
Hirschi, Ron. *Seya's Song.* (P, I) (A)
Houghton, Eric. *The Crooked Apple Tree.* (P, I)
Hume, Stephen Eaton. *Rainbow Bay.* (I)
Joosee, Barbara M. *I Love You the Purplest.* (I)
Katz, Karen. *Counting Kisses.* (P)
Lester, Alison. *Imagine.* (P, I)

Levinson, Ricki. *Our Home Is the Sea.* (I)
London, Jonathan. *Dream Weaver.* San Diego. (P, I)
London, Jonathan. *Into the Night We Are Rising.* (I)
London, Jonathan. *Like Butter on Pancakes.* (P, I)
London, Jonathan. *The Owl Who Became the Moon.* (I)
McFarlane, Sheryl. *Jessie's Island.* (P, I)
Nobisso, Josephine. *Shh! The Whale Is Smiling.* (I)
O'Neill, Mary. *Hailstones and Halibut Bones.* (P, I)
Pilkey, Dav. *The Paperboy.* (I)
Polacco, Patricia. *Appelemando's Dreams.* (I)
Ryder, Joanne. *Earthdance.* (I)
Ryder, Joanne. *Snail's Spell.* (P, I)
Slaughter, Hope. *A Cozy Place.* (P, I)
Thomson, Sarah. *Imagine a Day.* (I)
Thomson, Sarah. *Imagine a Night.* (I)
Udry, Janice May. *A Tree is Nice.* (P, I)
Van Laan, Nancy. *Little Fish Lost.* (P)
Van Laan, Nancy. *Rainbow Crow.* (P, I) (A)
Waboose, Jan Bourdeau. *Morning on the Lake.* (P, I) (A)
Wood, Douglas. *A Quiet Place.* (I)
Worth, Valerie. *All the Small Poems, Plus Fourteen More.* (P, I)

SEASONAL

Hundal, Nancy. *Camping.* (I)
Hundal, Nancy. *I Heard My Mother Call My Name.* (I)

Hundal, Nancy. *Prairie Summer.* (I)
Paolilli, Paul. *Silver Seeds.* (I)
Plourde, Lynn. *Spring's Sprung.* (P, I)
Plourde, Lynn. *Summer's Vacation.* (P, I)
Plourde, Lynn. *Winter Waits.* (P, I)
Robertson, M.P. *Seven Ways to Catch the Moon.* (I)
Ryan, Pam Munoz. *Hello Ocean.* (P, I)

WEATHER

Booth, David. *Voices in the Wind.* (I)
Brett, Jan. *The Umbrella.* (P, I)
Frasier, Debra. *Out of the Ocean.* (P, I)
Howell, Will C. *I Call It Sky.* (I)
Hundal, Nancy. *November Boots.* (P, I)
Tresslet, Alvin. *White Snow, Bright Snow.* (P, I)
Yolen, Jane. *Before the Storm.* (I)
Waboose, Jan Bourdeau. *Sky Sisters.* (P, I)
Zimmermann, Werner. *Snow Day.* (P, I)

MISCELLANEOUS

Brown, Margaret Wise. *The Color Kittens.* (P)
Browne, Anthony. *The Shape Game.* (I)
Fernandes, Eugenie. *Waves in the Bathtub.* (P)
Odor, Ruth. *My Quiet Book.* (P)
Piggot, Dawn. *Gregory and the Magic Line.* (P)
Thompson, Richard. *Then and Now.* (P)

Visualizing

Name: _____   Date: _____

1.	2.
3.	4.

I think the title of this book is _____

Using Our Senses

Name: _____   Date: _____

When I read the story _____ by _____ these are the . . .

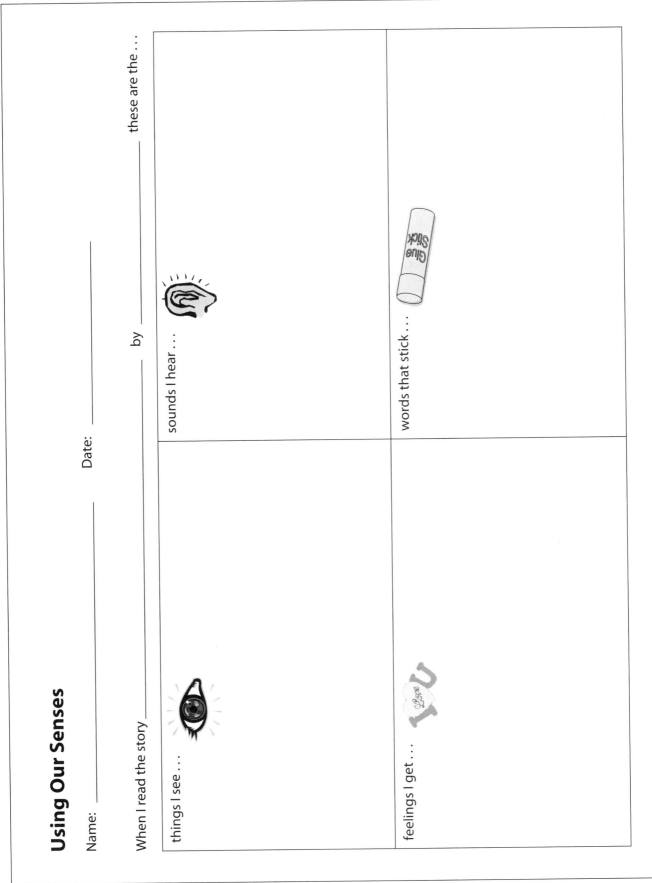

things I see . . .

sounds I hear . . .

feelings I get . . .

words that stick . . .

Visualize, Draw, and Reflect #1

Name: _____

Date: _____

Title: _____

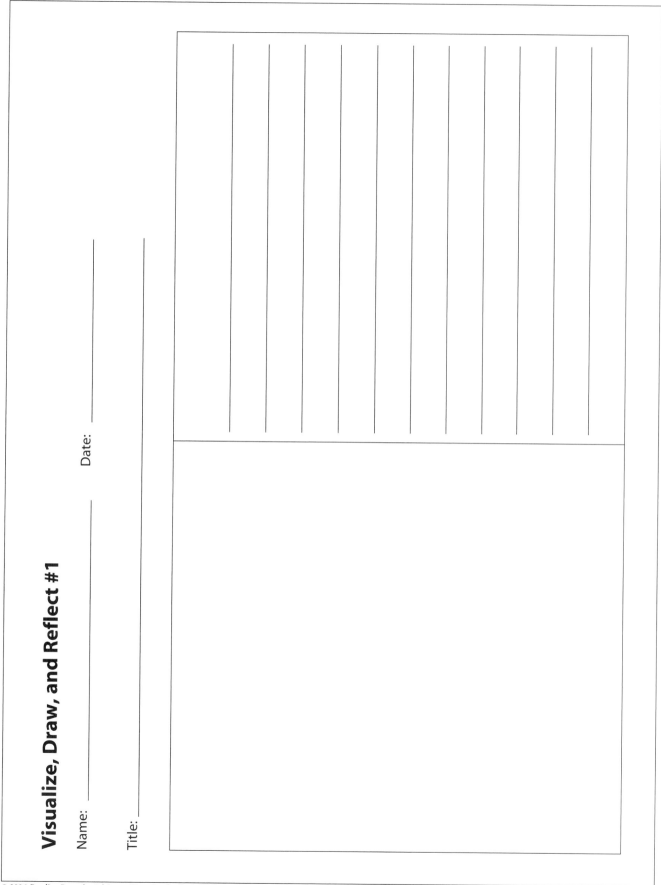

Visualize, Draw, and Reflect #2

Name: _____   Date: _____

When I read the story _____ by _____,

these are the pictures I see in my mind…

1.	2.
3.	4.

Visualizing During Reading

Name: _____   Date: _____

1. My image now . . .	2. . . .and now . . .
3. . . .and now . . .	4. . . .and now . . .

Listening for Picture Words

Name: _____   Date: _____

Title: _____   Author: _____

While you read . . .
Visualize the story. Use the author's words to help you make pictures in your mind.

After you read . . .
Draw one of the pictures that you visualized as you read. Around the picture, write the picture words (adjectives) the author used that helped you make the picture.

6 The Power to Infer

Infer Song
(to the tune of "My Bonnie Lies Over the Ocean")

Sometimes when you're reading a story
The words are not all there for you
So being a good book detective
Will help you to find any clue!

Chorus:
Infer! Infer!
Filling in what is not in the book!
Infer! Infer!
It's taking a much closer look!

Some authors leave clues in their pictures.
Some authors leave clues in their text.
They give you just part of their story
And want you to fill in the rest!

(Repeat Chorus)

So when you are reading a story
Be careful to read what is there
But then figure out what is missing—
Now you are inferring with flair!

✳ ✳ ✳

"Reading between the lines" has become the standard definition for inferring, but this has never been clear enough or concrete enough for me to really understand. Reading between the lines? What is that, exactly? The definition that I have found to be more helpful when teaching this strategy to children is this: Inferring is filling in, in your head, what is not written on the page. Just as the powers to Connect and Visualize are strongly linked, so is the Infer power linked to Question. The "in your head, not in the book" thinking that is introduced with deep-thinking questions is emphasized again with the strategy of inferring: drawing the readers' attention to the difference between what they know because the author has written it and what they need to "fill in" because the author did not include it.

I am often asked if inferring is the same strategy as predicting. Predicting is certainly a part of inferring, as a reader can "fill in" what they think might happen next in the story. But predicting what might happen next is only a part of what inferring encompasses and, while we need to include predicting in our teaching and modeling of this strategy, we need to go beyond it to the other aspects of "filling in" what is not directly in the text.

When readers learn to infer while reading:

- they learn to look for clues in text, in pictures, and in their own knowledge that will help them to make sense of the text.
- they are encouraged to become good "book detectives."
- they learn that some authors write very little text but leave clues for the reader to discover and interpret.
- they understand that the expression "less is more" means that fewer words on the page means more thinking for the reader.
- they are learning to fill in, in their heads, what's not written on the page.
- they are more likely to say, "Oh, I get it now!" while they read, than "Huh? I don't get it."

Introducing the Power to Infer

Inferring, because of its ties to higher-level thinking, is often a challenging concept for teachers to approach. How do we teach children to think beyond what is actually in the story? As with all the other reading powers and strategies, I believe that children know and are able to make inferences, but that what is going on in their heads has not yet been given a name or been made concrete. My five-year-old son Oliver, seeing the look on my face after he did something naughty, said, "Uh-oh. I'm inferring that I'm in trouble." Then, seeing my "look" quickly changing into a smile, said, "Oh, maybe I inferred wrong." I was smiling because it seemed odd for a five-year-old to be using the word "inferring" in proper context. What became clear to me was how easily Oliver was able to understand and use this language because I'm modeling it with him—not in a formal lesson, yet intentionally and purposefully integrating this language into his world every opportunity I could.

I like to help students unlock the mystery of inferring by telling them this:

I'm going to tell you a secret that will help you learn to infer. Are you ready? Here's the secret—not all authors tell you everything. But they didn't not tell you everything because they lost their pen or ran out of paper. They didn't tell you everything because they wanted you, the reader, to figure it out for yourself.

As with all the other reading powers, there are books that lend themselves best to teaching and practising the specific strategy. Books selected to teach visualizing, for example, have been specifically selected because of their rich language and detailed descriptions. But perhaps no other reading power relies quite so much on the specific literature used to model and teach it as inferring does. I believe that many of the books selected to support this strategy are written by perhaps the most talented authors. It is far more challenging to tell a story with few words—to imply rather than tell, to be subtle, to choose how much to actually say and just how much to leave out, to leak out a story in a controlled manner—than to tell everything at once. Authors such as Chris Van Allsburg, Anthony Browne, and David Wiesner are examples of writers who have mastered their craft. These writers tell their stories by *not* telling their stories. It is to these books and to these authors we turn when teaching students how to infer.

A few months ago, I made an interesting observation about the books I was using for some of these Reading Power Book Bins. While close to 80% of the books in the Visualize bin were had the writing and illustration done by different people, more than 80% of the books in the Infer bin were written and illustrated by the same person. Why is this? The answer has helped me understand inferring even more. I believe that the authors of the Infer books want to be in full control of both their stories and their pictures. They intentionally want to leak the story slowly and carefully onto the page. Having someone else illustrate their books would be giving up some of that control.

Another source for teaching readers to infer is wordless picture books, for what better source is there for "filling in, in your head" than a book with no or very few words? Books such as *Hug* by Jez Alborough, *Yo! Yes!* by Chris Raschka, or the *Good Dog Carl* series by Alexandra Day are perfect resources for helping students understand what inferring looks like and feels like. Children have no trouble "reading" the pictures to tell these stories; by naming the process Infer, we take what is already being done and make it tangible.

There was some controversy at my school a few years ago regarding comic books and graphic novels. Some parents and teachers felt that building up a large collection of comic books in the library promoted poor reading material for children. Our teacher-librarian, Lauren Smith, strongly disagreed. She knew that, while not all comic books are appropriate for school, the ones she was purchasing for the library, such as *Calvin and Hobbs* and *Garfield* were not only appropriate, but had reluctant readers, particularly boys, coming into the library on a regular basis and actually reading. In fact, she could rarely keep up with the demands of the students when it came to this genre. Still, the issues surrounding comic books remained. While some teachers forbade their students borrowing comics during book exchange, the comic books remained hidden in desks and between the pages of the Science textbook. Then Lauren came across an article about a small study conducted in the United States that found that boys who grew up reading comic books had, in fact, excelled in reading as they moved through high school and university. It was suggested that one of the reasons for this was that readers of comic books had already mastered the art of inferring. Comic books demand inferences between every frame. Readers of comic books might not be aware that what they are doing is called "inferring," but they would certainly be refining this skill by reading comic books on a regular basis. After Lauren shared this article with teachers and parents, the opinion about comic books shifted slightly and examples of this genre are now, more than ever, filling the shelves in our school library.

I agree that inferring is a challenging reading strategy to teach and practise. But by starting with simple texts and providing many opportunities for students to easily and successfully fill in parts of the story, we can reinforce the strategy and give this cognitive experience a name.

Sequential Lessons for Inferring

Lesson 1 (Teacher Directed/Group Participation): Games for Inferring

- Introduce the word "infer" and explain that inferring is something good readers do to try to figure out what the author is saying, even though the author may not have actually written it down. Explain that good readers are able to

"Less inking means more thinking."

One teacher used a page from a comic book to teach her students to infer. She copied one page from a comic book and cut out each frame. Then she glued the frames onto a long strip of white paper, leaving blank spaces between them. The students were to infer what was going on between each frame, and either draw or describe in writing what they thought the in-between frame might be.

infer because they look for clues in the pictures or the words to help them figure out what the book is about.

- **Game 1: Looking for Clues in Pictures**
Hold up a picture of a person showing an obvious emotion (the black and white photo-cards from *Second Step* work really well), or demonstrate an emotion yourself, and ask the students to try to infer what the person is feeling. Make sure you are showing facial expressions and body language. When someone guesses, ask them, "What were the clues that helped you infer that?" Try to get the students to be very specific. After repeating this a few times, have students come up and demonstrate their own emotions for the class to guess. Give feedback like "Great! You inferred that!" and "Good inference!" as much as possible.
- **Game 2: Looking for Clues in the Text** (adapted from Harvey & Goudvis, p. 106)
Choose one student to come to the front of the class. Explain that you are going to tape a card with an emotion (e.g., *disappointed*) written on it to the student's back. The class will give clues to help the student determine what emotion it is. In order to give a clue, the students need to think of a time when they actually felt that way, then phrase their clue like this: "I felt that way once when…" (e.g., "I felt that way once when I was hoping for something for my birthday, but I never got it"). The student at the front needs to listen to at least three clues before inferring the emotion.

Lesson 2 (Teacher Directed): Inferring from Wordless Books

- Explain to students that some books are written with no words at all, but that good readers can look for clues in the pictures and infer the story.
- Choose a wordless picture book and flip through the pages quickly. Say, "There are no words at all in this story. This story is told through the pictures (illustrations). I'm going to model how I look carefully at the clues in the picture and then infer what is going on."
- Turn to page one: "On this page, there is no writing, but there is a lot going on in the picture. I see… (describe what you see). Even though the author didn't write any words down, I can infer a lot from this picture. I infer… (make some inferences using "I think" or "Maybe")."
- Continue reading and modeling what you see and what you infer.
- Ask students to help: "Who can tell me what they see on this page?" "Who can infer what is happening?"
- Suggested books for this lesson are *Good Dog Carl* (and the rest of the Carl series) by Alexandra Day, *Pancakes for Breakfast* by Tomie DePaola, *The Red Book* or *Museum Trip* by Barbara Lahman. For older students, the wordless picture book *War* by Popov is exceptionally powerful, telling the story how wars are started and high the cost we pay for them. The story is told completely through illustrations, leaving the reader to infer the entire story. *Rose Blanche* by Robert Innocenti is another powerful book depicting the Nazi invasion through the eyes of a young Jewish girl.

Lessons 3–5 (Teacher Directed/Group Practice): Inferring from Very Little Text

- Books that use very little text to tell their stories are excellent for modeling and practising inferring. Explain to the students that some authors can write an entire story by using only one or two words. Usually these authors are also the il-

When modeling inferring, don't forget the title page and/or dedication page. Although we tend to skip these pages to get to the story, authors and illustrators often leave important clues there.

Wordless picture books are excellent starting points for teaching inferring because the reader needs to infer the entire text. Most readers do this automatically and naturally; in this lesson you are giving what they are doing a name.

lustrators, so they use their illustrations to tell the story. A good reader needs to look for clues in the illustrations to infer what the author *didn't* write.

- Begin to model. Show the title page or dedication page: "Now, there is no writing on this page, other than the title, but I'm going to be a good book detective and look carefully at this picture and make some inferences. On this page I can see… (describe some of the clues you see). I'm inferring that maybe… (model some inferences)."
- Continue this with the first few pages of the book, describing what you see in front of you, then making some inferences.
- After modeling three or four pages, ask if there is someone who would like to model inferring for the next page. Continue reading with different students modeling what they see and what they infer.
- Continue reading. Students share in partners what they see and what they infer.
- Writing extension: Have students choose one page of the book. Using the Talking and Thinking Bubbles template (page 33 or 91) they draw the picture and write the word from the book in the speech balloon, and write the inference in the thinking bubble.
- Suggested books for these lessons: *Hug* by Jez Alborough ("hug" is the only word in the book); *Oink!* by Karen J. Lammie; *Knuffle Bunny* by Mo Willems; *Yo! Yes!* and *Ring! Yo!* By Chris Raschka; *A Splendid Friend, Indeed* by Suzanne Bloom (great inferences can be made from the polar bear's expressions); and *Mama* by Jeannette Winter.

Lesson 6 (Independent Practice): Creating a Dialogue

- Remind students that some authors don't write everything, but will leave clues in their illustrations and elements of type to help their readers infer meaning.
- After reading the book *Yo! Yes!* by Chris Raschka, have students create a dialogue between two characters, using the Creating a Dialogue template on page 92. The criteria are that the dialogue is no longer than six exchanges, and that each character is allowed to say only one or two words per exchange.
- Students must provide clues for the reader to infer the meaning of the story, such as pictures or a change in text or font.
- Pairs of students can act out their dialogues for the class.
- In Chris Raschka's *Ring! Yo!*, the reader is given one end of a telephone conversation and must infer, from the clues in that person's comments and responses, what the conversation is about. At the end of the book, one possibility for the other side of the conversation is provided. Have students creating their own "other half" of the conversation, using the Telephone Conversation template on page 93. Two old telephones can become great props for when the class acts out these telephone calls.
- Suggested books for this lesson: *Yo! Yes!* and *Ring! Yo!* by Chris Raschka.

Pay attention to changes in text size and font. These are often clues left for the reader to help infer meaning.

Mama by Jeannette Winter is the true story of a baby hippo separated from his mother during the 2004 tsunami; *Owen and Mzee* by Isabella Hatkoff, a non-fiction account of this story, is a wonderful companion to the picture book.

The first time I did this lesson with a Grade 5 class, I got a great collection of "raps"— "Yo!" "Hey!" "Whaz up?" "Whaz happnin?" "Yo, man"—but none of them told a story. The challenge in this activity is to plan the story ahead of time so you can leave enough clues for the reader to infer a *story*.

I usually don't read Chris Raschka's version of the other side of the conversation until the students have been given time to write their own.

Lesson 7 (Guided Practice): Inferring from Clues

- Remind the students that sometimes authors intentionally leave clues for the reader throughout the book, providing information a little at a time to reveal a mystery at the end. A good reader will pay attention to the clues as they read and try to infer what the mystery is.
- Provide the students with the Inferring from Clues chart on page 94. Explain that you are going to read a story that gives clues but does not tell them right away about a mystery object.
- Begin by just reading the title: DO NOT show the students the cover or any illustrations. Using *Little Green*, by Keith Baker, ask students to infer just from that title what or who Little Green might be. Have them draw a picture and write the sentence in the first box. In partners, they can share their Little Greens with each other.
- Tell the students to listen carefully for the clues in the story to see if their Little Green fits or not. Stop reading, ask them to draw and write what they infer from the clues now. Is their Little Green fitting into the clues or do they need to change their Little Green? What were the clues that made them change their minds?
- Finish reading the story and ask students to make their final inference of what Little Green is. Reveal the cover and reread the story, showing the illustrations. Have students complete the last box.

If using *Little Green* or *Who is the Beast?* for this activity, have students complete the first section of their sheet before you read. They need to make their first inference from the title only. It is important, of course, not to show the students the cover of the book before reading the story.

- Suggested books for this lesson: *Little Green* or *Who Is the Beast?* by Keith Baker; *Seven Blind Mice* by Ed Young (seven blind mice all feel different parts of an elephant, trying to determine what "the thing" is; students listen to the clues of each of the mice to try to infer what the mice are feeling.)

Lesson 8 (Independent Practice): Inferring with Comics

Comic books demand the reader infer between the frames; therefore, children who are avid comic book readers often master the art of inferring and go on to become the high functioning readers.

- Photocopy a comic strip and cut out each frame separately. Glue the frames onto a long strip of white paper, leaving a blank frame between each comic frame.
- Have the students fill in—with words or pictures—what they think happened between each frame.
- Suggested comics for this lesson: *Garfield, Calvin and Hobbs.*

Lesson 9 (Teacher Directed): Inferring from Illustrations: O–W–I

If a student starts to describe what they see by saying "Well, maybe…," congratulate her or him on the inference.

- Choose an illustration that "tells a story" from a picture book. Show this picture to the class. On chart paper, make three column headings: What I **O**bserve, What I **W**onder, What I **I**nfer.
- Model to students how to complete the What I Observe column by looking carefully for clues in the picture and writing down a description of only what you can see. After modeling two or three illustrations, ask students to participate and record their responses on the chart paper. Use the opportunity to point out that, when someone says "Maybe" or "I think," they are actually making an inference. Write their comments in the third column.
- Complete the What I Wonder column by modeling your questions. Students can add their questions. Record their responses in the middle column.

One class I worked in this year liked this activity so much they decided to do an O–W–I once a week. Students started bringing in pictures from home that they wanted to use in the class.

- Complete the What I Infer column by telling the students that it is time for them to fill in what they think is going on in the picture. Model how an inference needs to begin with "I think…" or "Maybe…" to reinforce the notion that, when you make an inference, you are writing what you think based on your observation of the picture, not on what the author actually has written.

- Suggested books for this lesson: *Tight Times* by Barbara Shook Hazen, *Mysteries of Harris Burdick* or *The Sweetest Fig* by Chris Van Allsburg, *Tuesday* or *July 4, 1999* by David Wiesner, *Bootsie Barker Bites* by Barbara Bottner, *Tough Boris* by Mem Fox, *Owen and Mzee* by Isabella Hatkoff. This lesson works very well with real photographs taken from newspapers or non-fiction texts.

The portfolio edition of Chris Van Alsburg's *Mysteries of Harris Burdick* provides large illustrations on separate cards, perfect for a group O–W–I lesson.

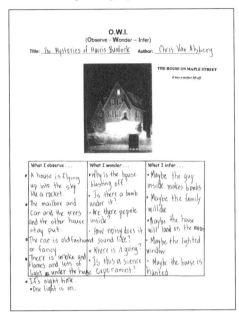

Lesson 10 (Independent Practice): O–W–I

- Choose an illustration from a book suggested for Lesson 9. Copy it into the box at the top of the O-W-I sheet on page 95.
- Students complete the O–W–I chart independently. Have student share their inferences with partners.
- Repeat this lesson, inviting students to find their own O–W–I illustration.

Lesson 11 (Teacher Directed): Inferring from Clues

Moving from illustrations into text is the "gradual release" that students need in order to feel confident and competent in their understanding of inferring and ability to infer.

- Review the game Looking for Clues in the Text on page 84. Remind students the secret of inferring: Not all authors tell you everything, and it's up to you, the reader, to look carefully at what the author did tell you, and then "fill in" what they didn't tell you.
- On chart paper, make three columns: Facts, Questions, Inferences.
- Choose a book from the Infer Booklist. (I find any of Anthony Brown's "Willy" books work well for this lesson.) Read the first page. In the first column, write down something that you know from the first page because the author actually wrote it. Model how you may be wondering something about that fact; write the question in the second column. Model an inference that answers the question—one that begins with "I think…" or "Maybe…"—and write it in the last column. Draw a line under your writing to indicate a new page.
- Continue modeling this with two or three more pages. Then ask the students to participate. Read a page and ask, "What do you know because the author actually wrote it?" Record their responses. Then move to the second column and ask, "What are you wondering about that?" Finally, record their answers to "What can you infer?" in the third column.

Inferring

Title: June 29, 1999

Author: David Wiesner

Facts	Questions	Inferences
• a girl launches vegetables into the sky	Why does she do that?	Maybe she wants to try something new.
• her classmates are speechless	why are they speechless?	I think they're amazed at what she did.
• a man sees giant turnips	why are the turnips so big?	Maybe they came from the balloons Holly sent off.
• Holly is puzzled	Why wasn't Arugula part of her experiment?	Maybe she never heard of arugula or she didn't plant

Lesson 12 (Independent Practice): Inferring from Text

- Students choose their own books. Supply students with Inferring from Text chart on page 96.
- Students complete chart, and share their inferences with the class or with partners.

> This way of reading, stopping, thinking, wondering, and inferring on paper is time consuming and not something I make students do every time they read. It is important to point out to students that what you are doing in this activity is *slowing down their thinking* so that they can see what an inference feels like and where it comes from. In real life reading experiences, inferences occur inside our heads, and sometimes they happen so quickly, we hardly notice them. Good readers, however, pay just as much attention to what authors *didn't* write as to what they *did* write.

Lesson 13: Reflective Journal

Have students record their thoughts about this new strategy and what they've learned about inferring. "How has inferring while you read helped you to understand the story better? Show me or tell me about your thinking."

Infer Booklist

Gems for Modeling Think-Alouds and Guided Practice

P = primary
I = intermediate
SR = social responsibility
A = Aboriginal

If we want our students to understand what inferring is, we need to show them what it looks like. It is important to spend the time modeling your own think-aloud inferences. here are some books for teachers to use for these modeling lessons.

Alborough, Jez. *Hug.* (P, I)
Baker, Keith. *Little Green.* (P, I)
Baker, Keith. *Who Is the Beast?* (P, I)
Bloom, Suzanne. *A Splendid Friend, Indeed.* (P)
Bottner, Barbara. *Bootsie Barker Bites.* (P, I)
Browne, Anthony. *Voices in the Park.* (I)
Browne, Anthony. *Willy the Wimp.* (I)
Browne, Anthony. *Willy the Wizard.* (I)
Browne, Anthony. *Zoo.* (I)
Davies, Jim. Any *Garfield* book. (P, I)
Day, Alexandra. *Carl Goes Shopping.* (P, I)
Day, Alexandra. *Good Dog Carl.* (P, I)
DePaola, Tomie. *Pancakes for Breakfast.* (P)
Ehlert, Lois. *Top Cat.* (P)
Fox, Mem. *Tough Boris.* (P, I)

Hazen, Barbara Shook. *Tight Times.* (P, I)
Innocenti, Roberto. *Rose Blanche.* (I)
Lahman, Barbara. *Museum Trip.* (P, I)
Lahman, Barbara. *The Red Book.* (P, I)
Lobel, Arnold. *Fables.* (I)
Marshall, James. *George and Martha.* (I)
Popov. *Why?* (I)
Raschka, Chris. *Ring! Yo!* (P, I)
Raschka, Chris. *Yo! Yes!* (P, I)
Rowe, Jeannette. *Whose Nose?* (P)
Van Allsburg, Chris. *The Garden of Abdul Gasazi.* (I)
Van Allsburg, Chris. *The Sweetest Fig.* (I)
Wiesner, David. *Tuesday.* (I)
Willems, Mo. *Knuffle Bunny* (P)
Young, Ed. *Seven Blind Mice.* (P, I)

Books for Independent Practice

P = primary
I = intermediate
SR = social responsibility
A = Aboriginal

Once the students are ready to practise inferring independently, they can choose books from the Infer bin. Choose from the following books to create a collection of Infer books for your classroom.

Browne, Anthony. *Into the Forest.* (I)
Browne, Anthony. *The Piggy Book.* (P, I)
Browne, Anthony. *Willy and Hugh.* (P, I)
Browne, Anthony. *Willy the Champ.* (P, I)
Browne, Anthony. *Willy the Dreamer.* (P, I)
Browne, Anthony. *Willy the Hero.* (P, I)
Burningham, John. *Aldo.* (P, I)
Burningham, John. *Come Away From the Water, Shirley.* (P, I)
Burningham, John. *Time to Get Out of the Tub, Shirley!* (P, I)
Heide, Florence Parry. *The Problem with Pulcifer.* (I)
Heide, Florence Parry. *The Shrinking of Treehorn.* (I)
Kasza, Keiko. *The Wolf's Chicken Stew.* (P, I)
Kimmel, Eric. *Pumpkin Head.* (P, I)
Kraft, Robert. *Chocolatina.* (P, I)
Lear, Munro. *Ferdinand.* (I)
McGugan, Jim. *Josepha – A Prairie Boy's Story.* (I)

McPhail, David. *Drawing Lessons from a Bear.* (P, I)
Marshall, James. *George and Martha: One Fine Day.* (I)
Marshall, James. *George and Martha: Rise and Shine.* (I)
Munson, Derek. *Enemy Pie.* (P, I)
Van Allsburg, Chris. *Jumanji.* (P, I)
Van Allsburg, Chris. *Just a Dream.* (P, I)
Van Allsburg, Chris. *The Mysteries of Harris Burdick* (regular or portfolio edition). (P, I)
Van Allsburg, Chris. *The Polar Express.* (P, I)
Van Allsburg, Chris. *The Stranger.* (P, I)
Van Allsburg, Chris. *The Widow's Broom.* (P, I)
Van Allsburg, Chris. *The Wretched Stone.* (P, I)
Van Allsburg, Chris. *Zathura.* (P, I)
Waddell, David. *Farmer Duck.* (P, I)
Wiesner, David. *Free Fall.* (I)
Wiesner, David. *Hurricane.* (I)
Wiesner, David. *June 29, 1999.* (P, I)
Wiesner, David. *The Three Pigs.* (P, I)

Talking and Thinking Bubbles

Name: _____   Date: _____

Title: _____   Author: _____

Creating a Dialogue

Name: _____   Date: _____

Title: _____

_____   _____

1	
2	
3	
4	
5	
6	

Telephone Conversation

Name: _____   Date: _____

_____	Yo?
_____	Hey!
_____	Uh huh.
_____	No.
_____	You?
_____	Oh.
_____	Mmm.
_____	So.
_____	And?
_____	What?
_____	You are?
_____	When?
_____	Um.
_____	Why?
_____	So what?
_____	Then?
_____	No?
_____	Yes.
_____	Never?
_____	Ever?
_____	You do?
_____	Me too!
_____	We will?
_____	I do!
_____	See?
_____	See.
_____	See ya!

Adapted from *Ring! Yo!* by Chris Raschka.

Inferring from Clues

Name: _____ Date: _____

Title: _____ Author:_____

I think _____ .

Now, I think _____ .

Now, I know _____ .

O–W–I

Name: _____   Date: _____

Title: _____   Author: _____

Place illustration here

What I **O**bserve	What I **W**onder	What I **I**nfer (begin with "I think . . ." or "Maybe")

Inferring from Text

Name: _____ Date: _____

Title: _____ Author: _____

Facts	Questions	Inferences

7 The Power to Transform

Transform Chant
Synthesize! Synthesize!
Transform your thinking
Let's synthesize!
Read a little, think a lot
Everyone tries
To make new meaning—
Let's synthesize!

Synthesize! Synthesize!
Transform your thinking
Let's synthesize!
Thinkin' starts a-changin'
Ideas start rearrangin'
You'll be surprised!
Just how easy
You can synthesize!

✳ ✳ ✳

When I first read the book *Miss Rumphius* by Barbara Cooney, I was transformed. I can honestly say that I changed the way I lived my life because of that book. In the story, young Alice tells her grandfather, whom she adores, that she wants to be just like him when she grows up: "When I grow up, Grandfather, I too will travel to far away places and then I will come home and live by the sea." But her grandfather reminds her that there is a "third thing" that she must do in her life: "to make the world more beautiful." In the story, Alice makes the world more aesthetically beautiful by scattering lupine seeds all around her village. For me, finding my own "third thing" became an important question: What was I going to do in my life to make the world a better place: what was I going to do to make a difference? I followed in Alice's footsteps and "traveled to far away places" when I taught in Japan for three years. Then I returned to Vancouver to "live by the sea." And my third thing? Well, I still don't know what my third thing is. And while I may not remember the names of the far-away places Alice traveled to or what color the lupines were that she planted, what I do remember from that story and what mattered to me most was the possibility of a "third thing"; an awareness and an openness to the possibility, and perhaps responsibility, to make the world a better place. This was my transformation. This was my mind sifting through the details of the story and connecting them to a meaningful whole—to what mattered most to me.

During the years I've spent teaching Reading Power to children and teachers, the strategies continue to evolve. This has been especially true of this last, and perhaps most complex, strategy. The word "transforming" has its roots in the strategy of synthesizing. In the early stages of developing this program, I lacked the

"A good book reaches deep inside and shakes the heart awake."
— Jean Little

Faye Brownlie also made reference at a recent leadership workshop to the dangers of a tight focus on comprehension.

"The good news is that comprehension instruction has become a long overdue reading focus. The bad news is that comprehension strategies and exercises often dominate comprehension instruction. Students are spending massive amounts of time learning and practicing these strategies, often without knowing how to apply them or not understanding how they fit into the big picture of reading."
— Regie Routman

courage to attempt to integrate the power to Synthesize because of my uncertainty of what it would look like in the classroom. I initially changed the name of the power to Transform because I believed it to be a word more familiar to children. Now, as the term "synthesize" is being used in upper-intermediate and high-school classrooms, I realize that teaching synthesizing strategies is a natural part of teaching the Transform power. The word "transform" refers to the notion that certain books can change the way we think about ourselves, about others, or about the world. Like synthesizing, it is an openness, a willingness, an awareness to sort through the details of a story and focus on those pieces that matter most to us. When we synthesize, we reorganize the story in terms of our own lives. Synthesizing, or transforming, combines and builds upon all four previous reading powers: it is the accumulation of the connections, the questions, the inferences, and the visual imagery combined to create the new thinking.

Several of my colleagues attended the International Reading Association's annual conference in Chicago in 2006. There was some interesting talk about some of the sessions they attended on recent trends and directions of comprehension instruction, a commonality of messages from leading educators in the field that I feel is worth noting. The overall message was that, if we continue to focus on comprehension strategies rather than critical thinking, we may be in danger of creating a dilemma we did not intend. By teaching comprehension strategies in isolation, our students may indeed learn to mirror what good readers do; however, if we isolate strategies solely for the purpose of comprehension, we are missing an important piece of critical thought. We need to be mindful of this, to continue to bring our students back to the "bigger picture"—the integrated whole, the structure and framework of critical thought. While we celebrate when our students begin to make connections or visualize, we cannot stop there. Moral ethic is created when we provide our students with opportunities to develop thinking, reasoning, and judgment skills through complex, real-world issues. Comprehension instruction must set the groundwork for critical thinking instruction.

In terms of Reading Power, it is imperative that we don't rest on our laurels when our students have mastered connecting, but that we continue teaching through the other strategies. Teaching Transform-the last Reading Power-and the moral issues introduced through specific books can be the first step towards laying the groundwork for critical thinking; it may lead our students towards a bigger context, providing them with a broader avenue to show their thinking.

I remember very clearly being taught the concept of summarizing: pulling out key ideas and rewriting them into a short paragraph "in my own words." These short paragraphs, as I recall, were to contain the key ideas of the piece, but my own thoughts or opinions were never to be included. Marks were taken off, in fact, if anything other than what was in the passage was included. While summarizing is the first step in synthesizing, it is certainly only a part of it. I now see summarizing as 2D (two-dimensional) reading—information from the text made smaller. But synthesizing can be interpreted as 3D reading—key points from the text, plus the reader's thinking to create a new thought (see Synthesis diagram on page 107.) When we synthesize, we add another layer to our reading: that other layer is our thinking, our background knowledge, and our experiences. This was the layer that I was discouraged from including in my summary paragraphs in high school, but the layer I now cannot imagine omitting from my teaching.

When readers learn to be transformed by what they read:

- they understand that books have the ability to change the way we think about ourselves and our world.
- they can be touched in some way by the words on the page, the thoughts in their heads, and the feelings in their hearts.
- they are introduced to books that deal with thought-provoking issues: war, conservation, homelessness, social responsibility, the integrity of the human spirit, poverty, the rights of children.
- they learn to look beyond the pages of the text towards the implications and effects the book may have on their own lives.
- they are challenged by change.
- they understand that transformation takes place over time, and that reading a particular book plants seeds that may one day make a difference to the way they live or view the world.
- they know that a story has the power to change them, because their brains have the power to store away facts, stories, questions, and feelings that will shape their lives.
- they learn to look for the things in a book that matter most to them.
- they ask themselves, "What difference has this book made to me?" or "Has anything in me changed because of this book?"
- they are learning that being able to identify what matters to them is the beginning of being shaped by the world around them.

Introducing the Power to Transform

In order to teach this complex strategy to children, we turn, once again, to the appropriate literature as a starting point. There are, as with all the Reading Powers, particular books that lend themselves well to this strategy. These are the books that offer readers opportunities to find the meaningful pieces hidden amongst the details of the story. (Often a few tissue boxes are required or reading!) These messages are sometimes very obvious, as in *Ordinary Mary's Extraordinary Deed*, and sometimes less so, as in *The Dot*.

While some may see transforming as a complex strategy, I have noticed how naturally children begin to interpret and infuse the details of their own lives with the highlights of the text to find embedded meaning. I was teaching a Transform lesson in a Grade 4 classroom and modeled my thinking using the book *Ish* by Peter H. Reynolds, the story of a young artist whose creativity is suddenly halted by the stinging words of his older brother, but who is helped to regain his confidence by his sister's view of his art. After reading and filling out the Reading Voice/Thinking Voice chart (see page 108), I shared with the students my synthesis for the story:

> I think this story is about how sometimes what we say and what we do can have a tremendous impact on other people. I remember feeling very insecure about myself in elementary school because people used to make fun of me because I wore dresses. Their cruel words, just like those of Raymond's brother, affected me. This book reminded me how powerful words can be—both in a negative way and in a positive way.

I then reminded the students that, just as all of us are different, our syntheses of a story can also differ. I asked if anyone had a different synthesis that they would like to share. One boy put up his hand and said "I think the book is about how sometimes you need to go to a bad place before you can get to the good place. The thing I'm taking from this book is that even when I feel terrible and think my life sucks, it's gonna get better eventually."

I was overwhelmed. "Wow," I choked, holding back tears. "You have synthesized far beyond what I did and you have helped make this book even more meaningful for me. Thank you." If I ever had doubts about children being capable of synthesizing, that nine-year-old boy put them to rest.

In my position as workshop presenter, it is important for me to give teachers a clear picture of a strategy so that they not only understand it, but can easily apply it to their practice. The Transform strategy proved challenging for me in this respect because of the complexity of the idea of synthesis. Stephanie Harvey states, "synthesizing involves combining new information with existing knowledge to form an original idea, a new line of thinking, or a new creation" (1998, p. 137). However, I needed more than a definition if I was to be teaching teachers to teach students what the strategy really looks like. For concrete examples, I found it helpful to refer to two everyday objects—a synthesizer and synthetic fabric—both of which are named from the same root word. A synthesizer combines different musical instruments to create a new sound. Synthetic fabric combines different materials to create a new material. A good reader combines information from text with background knowledge to create a new idea or thought.

When introducing the Power to Transform to students, I explain that the another word for transform is "synthesize." I give the real-life examples of synthesis; e.g., musical synthesizer and synthetic fabric. With older students, I talk about the difference between summary and synthesis: summary as two-dimensional reading and synthesizing as three-dimensional reading, or adding the "thinking layer" to your reading.

With younger students, I simplify this by explaining that sometimes when we read a book, there is a an important message that the author didn't actually write, but wants us to think about after we finished the story.

Passing out piles of LEGO pieces to groups and inviting them to "transform" the pieces into something new provides a concrete visual for the concept. Noticing that each group arranged their pieces in a different way helps to illustrate that there is no "one way" to synthesize text.

Sometimes, after I read a story, I wish that the author had written me a special message at the back of the book.

(I turn to the back page and pretend to read)

"Dear Ms. Gear. After you have finished reading this book, these are the thoughts that I would like you to take away with you…. Here is the important message that I want you to remember from this book…."

(I turn the book to show the blank page)

The author didn't actually write me a special message to me. But as a good reader, I know that it's important to spend some time thinking about the book after I finished reading; I want to think to myself, *What part of this story "sticks"?*

> I always read Barbara Cooney's *Miss Rumphius* to model my "change in thinking."

> Now I'm finished this story and I'm going to put it away. But after I put it away, there are some new thoughts that I have in my head that I didn't have before. This book really changed my thinking a lot. In the book, Miss Rumphius made the world more beautiful by planting lupine seeds around her town. The important thing I took from that book is that one person can make a difference in the world. Now I am always wondering about what I can do in my life that could make a difference to the world or to other people. I may not plant lupine seeds, but I'm going to try to do something to make a difference. If I had never read this book before, I may not have ever had this thought. My thinking changed because of this book. That is what transforming is.

Sequential Lessons for Transforming

Lesson 1 (Teacher Directed): A Change in Thinking

- Spend time explaining the concept of Transform—a change in thinking. Describe how reading can change the way we think and can help us create new ideas and new thoughts. The ideas from the book plus the thoughts in our heads equal Transform.
- Share the Synthesis diagram on page 107.
- Model how a book that has made an impact on you has changed your thinking in some way.
- After you have finished reading, model a synthesis of the theme or message of the story (see box above).
- Suggested books to use to model "a change in thinking": *Miss Rumphius* by Barbara Cooney (making a difference); *Scaredy Squirrel* by Melanie Watt (courage, taking risks); *The Gift of Nothing* by Patrick McDonnell (the gift of companionship); *Ordinary Mary's Extraordinary Deed* by Emily Pearson (random acts of kindness); *Mr. Peabody's Apples* by Madonna (consequences of telling a false rumor about someone); *The Invisible Mistakecase* by Charise Mericle Harper (value of learning through making mistakes).

"Our thinking can actually change or transform while we read. Good readers sometimes take what they have read plus their thinking voice to create a new thought. It is like adding another layer to your reading—the thinking layer."

Lessons 2–3 (Teacher Directed): Finding the Important Message

- This lesson provides a stepping stone for students to begin to notice what matters in a story by reading a book with a very obvious message—making a difference
- Tell the students you will read a book to them, and that you are going to see how this book has transformed (changed) their thinking. Remind them that transforming, or synthesizing, is paying attention to your thinking while you read and then finding what mattered to them in the story.
- Choose a book in which the important message is how we can make a difference. Read the book aloud. Afterwards, have the students find a partner and discuss: What did the character in this story do to make a difference in the world? How might this story change your thinking? What could you do to make a difference?
- Come together as a class to share. Have students complete the Making a Difference sheet on page 109.

Students may or may not expand their thinking on paper, but always allow time for discussing how the character made a difference.

The My Extraordinary Deed web on page 110 is specifically designed to be used with the book *Ordinary Mary's Extraordinary Deed* by Emily Pearson; however, it can be used with other books from this lesson.

- Suggested books for this lesson: *Ordinary Mary's Extraordinary Deed* by Emily Pearson, *The Teddy Bear* by David McPhail, *Miss Rumphius* by Barbara Cooney, *Sophie's Masterpiece* by Eileen Spinelli, *Stone Soup* by Jon Muth, *The Dot* by Peter H. Reynolds, *The Peace Book* by Todd Parr.

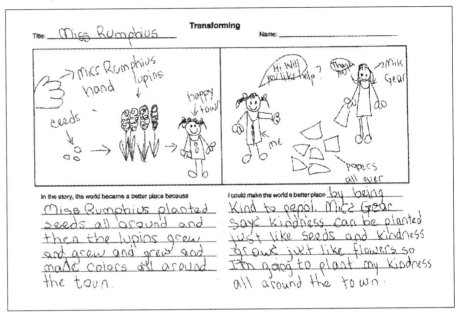

Lessons 3–5 (Teacher Directed/Student Participation): Thinking Changes as We Read

- Explain to students that sometimes when we start a book, we have ideas or thoughts about what the book is about, but while we read our thinking changes. At the end of the story, our thinking may be completely different from when we first started to read.
- Choose a book from the list below. Books that have unexpected or surprise endings work well for this lesson. Pass out one of the Noticing How My Thinking Changes charts on pages 111 and 112.
- Read the first few pages of the book. Stop and have the students fill in the first box. Invite students to share their ideas with the class or in partners.
- Continue reading through the rest of the story. Have the students fill out the middle box on the sheet, and share with partners.
- Explain how the last box is similar to the work they have been doing in previous lessons: What from this story is your "new thought" (an idea or thought that you have now but may not have had before you heard this story)?
- Suggested books for this lesson: *Oi! Get Off Our Train* by John Burningham, *First Day Jitters* by Julie Danneberg, *Where Once There Was a Wood* by Denise Flemming.

Lesson 6 (Teacher Directed): Modeling Looking for What Matters Most

This lesson can also be done using Looking For What Matters Most chart on page 113.

- Choose a book that can be modeled as having an important message or impact on your life; a book with which you can model your "transformed thought."
- Create a chart based on the Reading Voice/Thinking Voice template on page 108. On one side, you are going to write a short summary of what has happened up to a certain place in the story. On the other side, you are going to record your thinking voice.

- Begin to read aloud and stop after every few pages, recording your reading voice (summary) and your thinking voice on the chart paper.
- Try to model short summaries on the left and longer responses on the right. Draw students' attention to this: "I notice that my summary is quite short and that's okay. In fact, I'm not as interested in this side, because it's basically retelling what I've already read. What I am more interested in is the right side, because this is the window into a reader's thinking. This is what's going to tell me how well you understand your thinking and are using your Reading Powers. So I'm going to be looking for lots of writing on this side of the page, when you are working on this on your own."
- After you have finished reading, explain that synthesis is an ART—**A**fter **R**eading **T**hought. The thinking voice has helped you keep track of your thoughts while you were reading and now it's time to reflect on the meaning of the story more deeply.
- Model your synthesis of the book: "After reading and thinking about this book, I now want to add these two columns together and look at my new thoughts. What mattered most to me in this story? What part is going to stick with me long after I put the book away?" Remind the students that, because we are all different, what matters to one person may be different from what matters to another.
- Suggested books for this lesson: *Miss Rumphius* by Barbara Cooney (making a difference); *Scaredy Squirrel* by Melanie Watt (courage, taking risks); *The Gift of Nothing* by Patrick McDonnell (the gift of companionship); *Ordinary Mary's Extraordinary Deed* by Emily Pearson (random acts of kindness); *Mr. Peabody's Apples* by Madonna (consequences of telling a false rumor about someone); *A Color of His Own*, or *Frederick*, or *Alexander and the Wind Up Mouse* by Leo Lionni; any of the short stories in *Zen Shorts* by Jon Muth.

Lessons 7–8 (Guided Practice): How Reading Can Change Your Thinking

- This lesson is similar to Lesson 6, but the students are now completing the sheet on their own.
- Pass out Reading Voice/Thinking Voice template on page 108 to students. Begin reading a story aloud, pausing after every few pages. Have students write their summary on the left column and their thinking voice on the right. Allow time for sharing.
- When the story is finished and the students have completed both sides of their chart, explain that you want them to try to synthesize their thoughts and ideas about the book: "Now it is time to show me what matters most to you from this story. What new thoughts do you have? I don't want you to retell the story to me because I just finished reading it—I want to know what you are thinking and what you will remember most about it. What matters to you?"
- After they have completed the My Transformed Thoughts box, invite students to share their ideas with each other or with the class.
- Suggested book for this lesson: *The Araboolies of Liberty Street* by Sam Swope, *The Teddy Bear* by David McPhail, *Faithful Elephants* by Yukio Tsuchiya, *Sophie's Masterpiece* by Eileen Spinelli, *The Dot* or *Ish* by Peter H. Reynolds, *The Three Questions* by Jon Muth, any book by Leo Lionni.

Synthesizing is an A.R.T.—an After Reading Thought.

"Now that I've finished reading the author's story and the book has been put aside, what am I thinking about? What is my after reading thought?"

Reading a story can sometimes change the way we think about ourselves, think about the world, or think about other people.

Title: Ish   Author: Peter Reynolds

So far: What the author said in the story...	My Thinking Voice: My reaction/response: (What I'm thinking, wondering, feeling...)
• Ramon liked to draw, and one day Ramon tried to draw the flower in the vase exactly the same.	• I like to draw exactly the same when I am bored and when I have plenty of time. *great description*

Synthesis:
My new thoughts: What the author did not say, but now I'm thinking about
(The part that "sticks")

I think its important to listen to yourself whats right to do, if somebody is wrong and mean. ✓

Powerful effort.

Lessons 9–11 (Independent Practice): Showing How Books Change Your Thinking

- Have the students choose their own books from the Transform Book Bin and fill out either Reading Voice/Thinking Voice (page 108) or Looking for What Matters Most (page 113) independently.
- Have students share their synthesis of the books with the class.

Lesson 12 (Guided Practice): Looking for Common Themes

- This lesson teaches students to pay attention to the big idea or themes from the books. Explain that the books they are choosing from were chosen particularly because of the message the author has left.
- Brainstorm some of the themes that students have started to notice from the books.
- Create a class grid of themes and have students record titles under each theme. Some books will, of course, fall under several categories (see table on page 105).

THEME	BOOK TITLE
War	*The Cello of Mr. O*
	Faithful Elephants
	Sami and the Times of the Troubles
	Feathers and Fools
	The Upstairs Cat
Death and/or the Circle of Life	*Peach and Blue*
	Prince of Butterflies
	Sophie's Masterpiece
	The Memory String
	When the Wind Stops
	The Great Change
	(see also books listed on p. 44, Loss of Loved One)
Conservation (Animal and Environment)	*Where Once There Was a Wood*
	The Great Kapok Tree
	Hey! Get Off Our Train
	My Friend Whale
Peace	*Somewhere Today – A Book of Peace*
	The Peace Book
	Whoever You Are
	The Araboolies of Liberty Street
	A Poppy Is to Remember
Making a Difference	*Miss Rumphius*
	Finding the Green Stone
	The Teddy Bear
	Ordinary Mary's Extraordinary Deed
	The Three Questions
	Stone Soup
	The Dot
	Painted Words/ Spoken Memories

Lesson 13: Reflective Journal

Have students record their thoughts about this new strategy and what they've learned about transforming. "How has transforming while you read helped you to understand the story better? Show me or tell me about your thinking."

Transform Booklist

Gems for Modeling Think-Alouds and Guided Practice

P = primary
I = intermediate
SR = social responsibility
A = Aboriginal

If we want our students to understand what transforming is, we need to show them what it looks like. It is important to spend time modeling your own think-aloud transformations. Here are some books for teachers to use for these modeling lessons.

Aliki. *Painted Words/Spoken Memories.* (SR) (P, I)

Brumbeau, Jeff. *The Quilt Makers Gift.* (SR) (I)

Burningham, John. *Hey! (Oi!) Get Off Our Train!* (SR) (I)

Condra, Estelle. *See the Ocean.* (I)

Cooney, Barbara. *Miss Rumphius.* (P, I)

Costanzo, Charlene. *The Twelve Gifts of Birth.* (I)

Evyindson, Peter. *Red Parka Mary.* (SR) (P, I) (A)

Fleming, Denise. *Where Once There Was a Wood.* (SR) (P)

Kilborne, Sarah. *Peach and Blue.* (P, I)

Lovell, Patty. *Stand Tall, Molly Lou Melon.* (SR) (P)

Madonna. *Mr. Peabody's Apples.* (SR) (I)

McDonnell, Patrick. *The Gift of Nothing.* (P, I)

McPhail, David. *The Teddy Bear.* (SR) (P, I)

Muth, Jon. *The Three Questions.* (I)

Pearson, Emily. *Ordinary Mary's Extraordinary Deed.* (SR) (P, I)

Reynolds, Peter H. *The Dot.* (SR) (P, I)

Reynolds, Peter H. *Ish.* (SR) (P, I)

Swope, Sam. *The Araboolies of Liberty Street.* (I)

Tsuchiya, Yukio. *Faithful Elephants: The True Story of Animals, People and War.* (I)

United Nations. *For Every Child.* (I)

Watt, Melanie. *Scaredy Squirrel.* (P, I)

White Deer of Autumn. *The Great Change.* (I) (A)

Wilson, Troy. *The Perfect Man.* (P, I)

Books for Independent Practice

P = primary
I = intermediate
SR = social responsibility
A = Aboriginal

Once the students are ready to practise transforming independently, they can choose books from the Transform bin. Choose from the following books to create a collection of Transform books for your classroom

Baylor, Byrd. *The Table Where Rich People Sit.* (P, I) (A)

Bruchac, Joseph. *A Boy Called Slow.* (I) (A)

Bunting, Eve. *The Memory String.* (I)

Bunting, Eve. *Riding the Tiger.* (I)

Cherry, Lynn. *The Great Kapok Tree.* (I)

Coville, Bruce. *Prince of Butterflies.* (I)

Crow, Allan. *The Crying Christmas Tree.* (P, I) (A)

Cutler, Jane. *The Cello of Mr. O.* (I)

Downey, Roma. *Love Is a Family.* (P, I)

Eyvindson, Peter. *Jen and the Great One.* (SR) (P, I) (A)

Fitzpatrick, Marie-Louise. *The Long March: The Choctaw's Gift to Irish Famine Relief.* (I) (A)

Fleischman, Paul. *Weslandia.* (I)

Fox, Mem. *Feathers and Fools.* (I)

Fox, Mem. *Whoever You Are.* (P, I)

Fox, Mem. *Wilfred Gordon Macdonald Partridge.* (P, I)

Goldin, Barbara Diamond. *The Girl Who Lived with the Bears.* (I) (A)

Heide, Florence Parry. *Sami and the Time of the Troubles.* (P, I)

James, Simon. *My Friend Whale.* (P, I)

Kuskin, Karla. *The Upstairs Cat.* (SR) (P, I)

Lewis, Paul Owen. *Grasper.* (P, I)

Lionni, Leo. *Frederick.* (P, I)

Lucado, Max. *You Are Special.* (I)

McCaughrean, Geraldine. *My Grandmother's Clock.* (I)

Morrison, Toni. *The Big Box.* (P, I)

Munsch, Robert. *The Paper Bag Princess.* (P, I)

Muth, Jon. *Stone Soup.* (SR) (P, I)

Muth, Jon. *Zen Shorts.* (I)

Myers, Christopher. *Wings.* (I)

Parr, Todd. *The Peace Book.* (P, I)

Pinkwater, Daniel Manus. *The Big Orange Splot.* (P, I)

San Souci, Robert. *Nicholas Pipe.* (I)

Polacco, Patricia. *The Bee Tree.* (P, I)

Silverstein, Shel. *The Giving Tree.* (P, I)

Spinelli, Eileen. *Sophie's Masterpiece.* (I)

Taylor, C.J. *The Secret of the White Buffalo.* (I) (A)

Thomas, Shelley Moore. *Somewhere Today: A Book of Peace.* (P, I)

Vaughan, Richard Lee. *Eagle Boy.* (SR) (P, I) (A)

Walker, Alice. *Finding the Green Stone.* (SR) (P, I)

Walsh, Melanie. *My World, Your World.* (P)

Zolotow, Charlotte. *When the Wind Stops.* (P, I)

Synthesis

Name: _____

Date: _____

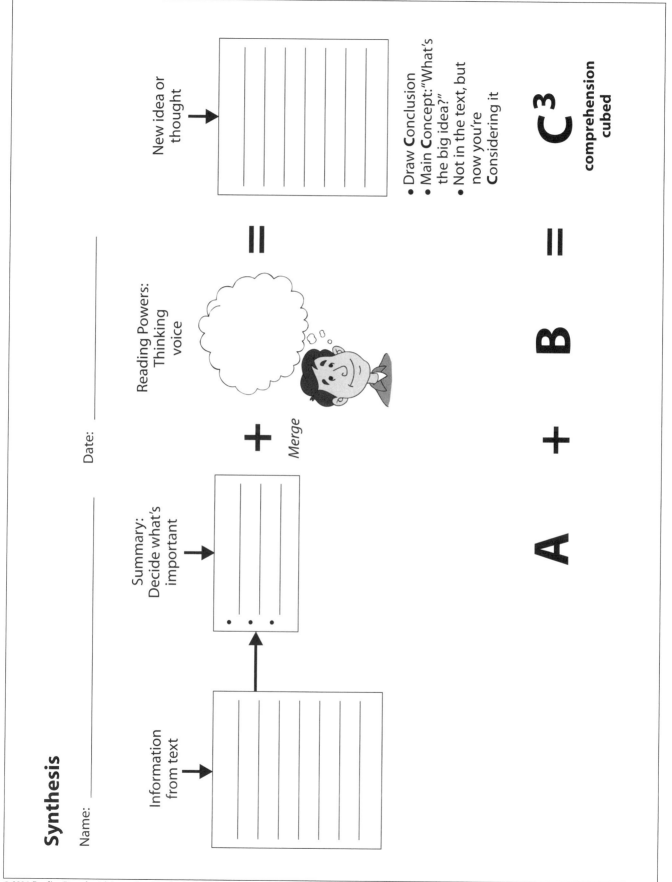

Information from text →

Summary: Decide what's important →

+

Merge

Reading Powers: Thinking voice

=

New idea or thought →

- Draw **C**onclusion
- Main **C**oncept: "What's the big idea?"
- Not in the text, but now you're **C**onsidering it

A + B = C³

comprehension cubed

Reading Voice/Thinking Voice

Name: _____

Date: _____

Title: _____

Author: _____

My Reading Voice	My Thinking Voice
So far in the story . . . (Summary of what the author wrote)	My connections, questions, inferences, visual images, thoughts, reactions, feelings, etc.
My Transformed Thoughts What is not written in the story, but now I'm thinking about . . . . (The part that "sticks")	

Making a Difference

Title: _____

Name _____

In the story, the world is a better place because . . .

_____
_____
_____
_____
_____
_____
_____

I could make the world a better place by . . .

_____
_____
_____
_____
_____
_____
_____

My Extraordinary Deed

Name: _____

Date: _____

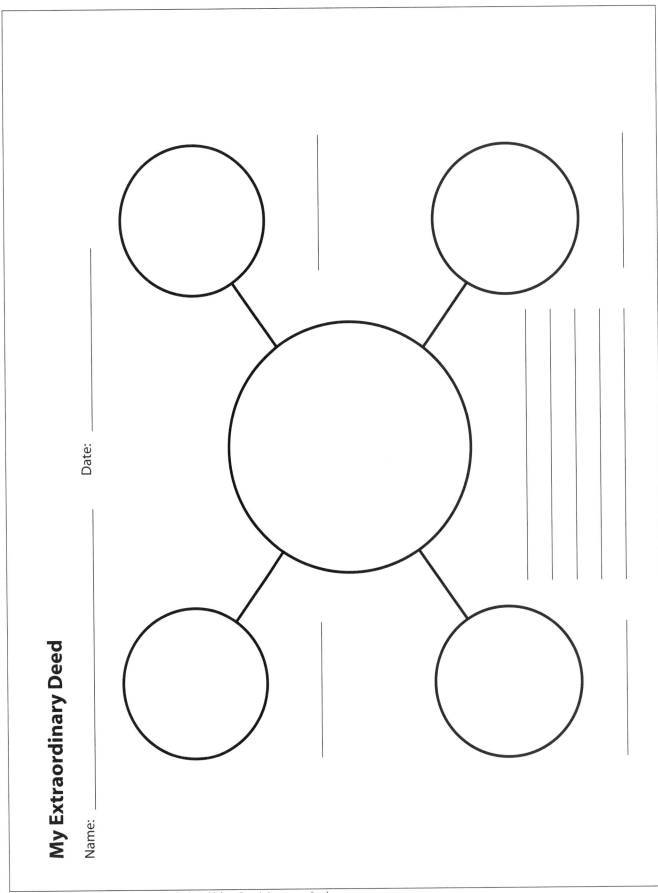

Noticing How My Thinking Changes #1

Name: _____   Date: _____

Title: _____   Author: _____

My first thought…

On second thought…

My transformed thought…

Noticing How My Thinking Changes #2

Name: _____   Date: _____

Title: _____   Author: _____

At first I thought…

But then I wondered. . .

Then I understood…

Looking for What Matters Most

Name: _____   Date: _____

Title: _____   Author: _____

The "big idea" in this book is…

_____

_____

_____

_____

My thoughts, ideas and opinions about _____ before reading:

_____

_____

_____

_____

But I've changed my mind. Now I think…

_____

_____

_____

_____

What matters most to me is…

_____

_____

_____

_____

8 Application and Assessment

Application

After students become familiar with all five Reading Power strategies, they are ready to apply their "busy brains" to any book. Many books, I have discovered, lend themselves well to all strategies, and while I have suggested isolating these strategies to teach them, it is also important to model how a good reader is able to use all five strategies intermittently while they read. Most books in the Transform Bin could be used to practise the different strategies or powers with a single book.

Using the Reading Powers

C – if you make a connection
Q – if you asked a question
V – if the passage was descriptive and you were able to visualize
I – if you found yourself thinking: "Well, maybe…." Or "I think…."
T – if you notice your thinking changing

The Double-Entry Journal on page 115 is an excellent way to have students practise using these strategies while they read: one side of the page is a summary of what they know so far from reading the book, while the other side is used to record their thinking voice. Older and more competent readers could begin to code their thinking voice by marking their thoughts with the letters of the strategies used.

The Using My Reading Powers grid on page 116 is another way for students to demonstrate their understanding of several different reading powers using one book.

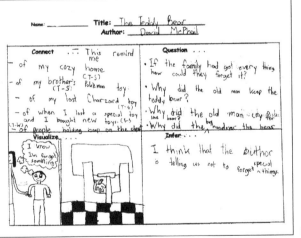

Grade 3 Sample

Combined Reading Powers Booklist

These books are suggested for practising several strategies at once.

Aliki. *Painted Words/ Spoken Memories*
Estelle Condra. *See the Ocean*
David McPhail. *The Teddy Bear*
Jon Muth. *The Three Questions*
Jon Muth. *Zen Shorts*
Sam Swope. *The Araboolies of Liberty Street*
White Deer of Autumn. *The Great Change*

Double-Entry Journal

Name: _____   Date: _____

Title: _____   Topic: _____

Facts So far in the story… (Summary of what the author wrote)	**My Thinking Voice** My reaction/response… (What I'm thinking, wondering, feeling, etc.)

Using My Reading Powers

Name: _____   Date: _____

Title: _____   Author: _____

My connections	My questions
What I visualized	**My inferences**

My transformed thought

Using Reading Power with Novels

Literature circles or novel studies are excellent opportunities for older students to utilize and practise their reading powers with more complex texts. While my past experience literature circles had not proven very successful, Reading Power has allowed me to "fine tune" the structure of the literature circle so that students became more engaged in the reading, thinking, and discussing of the books. Students who have been exposed to the language of thinking, by learning and practising the Reading Power strategies with picture books, can then use these strategies with more sophisticated texts. Their literature circles look, sound, and feel more like legitimate book-club discussions, rather than the forced talk that tend to come from the assigned roles traditional to literature circles.

While they read the novels, students use lined sticky notes to record their thinking voices. These can be then peeled off and stuck into a journal or notebook, with the chapter number recorded at the top of the page. These sticky notes represent a student's thinking and understanding of the novel far better, in my opinion, than answering questions on each chapter or making a "product" type of extension ("And now we will make a diorama..."). For discussion sessions, students need to come to their lit circle prepared to share one of the passages from the chapter where their thinking voice "was the loudest." One at a time, students in the group read their selected passage aloud and explain their thinking to the group. More proficient readers may also be able to identify which strategy they used. Other students in the group can then contribute their own comments or thoughts to the discussion. If two students have chosen the same passage, a comparison of "thinking" can be part of the discussion.

Here are some examples from a group of Grade 4 students who were discussing the novel *Stone Fox* by John Reynolds Gardiner:

- "When I read this part, I made it reminded me of the time that my grandpa was very sick and he had to go to the hospital. He couldn't get out of bed and it made me feel so scared and sad all mixed together." (Connect)
- "When I read this part, it made really clear pictures in my mind. The words that really helped me create my pictures were…. I drew a picture of it." (Visualize)
- "When I read this part I was thinking that maybe Willy would change his mind about entering the dog sled race after he saw Stone Fox's team. That was an inference, I think, because my brain said "maybe." (Inference)
- "When I read this part, I was really confused. I mean, how could Willy actually think that he would win when he only had one dog and everyone else had a whole team of dogs?" (Question)

> ### Literature Circles provides an opportunity for students
>
> - to apply their Reading Powers to exciting novels
> - to actively engage with the text
> - to become metacognitive readers
> - to share in rich, personal, meaningful discussions about the books with their peers
> - to extend their thinking into writing activities

Allowing students to choose already familiar charts and templates (Blackline Masters or BLMs) to extend their thinking on paper is another means to encourage application of these strategies, and provides them with different ways to show their thinking.

Students read aloud their selected passage directly from the novel first and then share their thinking.

Lessons for Literature Circles

INTRODUCING THE POWERS

- Provide direct instruction in Reading Power (comprehension strategies) using picture books
- Divide your class into three or four groups based on reading ability as seen by assessment.
- Set at least two one-hour blocks per week for literature circles:
  - Block 1: R–T–R (Read, Think, Respond)
  - Block 2: SPOT (Sharing Passages & Our Thinking)
- Choose an appropriate novel for each group. Read the novels ahead of time.
- Provide each student with a copy of the novel, a notebook, and lined sticky notes. The notebooks will hold their "thinking" and various writing extensions.

FIRST SESSIONS

- Have the other groups occupied while you visit one group.
- Model the first chapter (or pages) of the novel using read-aloud/think-aloud strategy and marking your thinking voice on sticky notes.
- Model the selection of a passage where your "thinking voice was the loudest."
- Repeat this modeling with the other groups.

Lit Circle Snapshot

Once the routines have been established, your lit circles may look like this:

BLOCK 1: R–T–R (READ, THINK, RESPOND)

- all students reading their own novels silently and marking their thinking voices
- some may be working on writing extensions using Reading Power BLMs
- teacher posts the chapter each group will be discussing during the next SPOT — all students are responsible for having completed that chapter

BLOCK 2: SPOT (SHARING PASSAGES & OUR THINKING)

- students meet in lit circle groups (desks moved to create groups)
- students come prepared to share one passage from the chapter and their thinking connected to that passage
- student take turns reading their passages out loud and sharing their thoughts
- after each turn, others respond
- teacher visits groups, modeling his or her own passage and thinking for that chapter, and listening/guiding conversation
- teacher may or may not use this visit to explain a writing extension with using a BLM

Remember...

- Students may read at their own pace.
- Chapters being discussed are posted one or two days before the SPOT session.
- "Thinking" sticky notes are peeled off and placed in notebooks. Notebook pages should have a heading with chapter and page numbers so that you know which part of the novel the thinking came from. ***This is important evidence into the students' thinking***

- Most advanced group(s) are "gradually released" from writing all thinking voices, and are responsible for coming to their lit circle with only the passage and thinking they are planning to share.
- Students choose their own BLMs to show their thinking.

Recommended Books for Lit Circles

Grade 3

Lynne Reid Banks, *Harry the Poisonous Centipede*

Barbara Fienburg, *Tashi* (fantasy, curiosity, adventure)

Sara Pennypacker, *Stuart Goes To School* (worrier, school adventure)

Jill Tomlinson, *The Owl Who Was Afraid of the Dark*

Grade 4

Anne Fienberg, *Horrendo's Curse* (courtesy, pirates, adventure)

John Reynolds Gardiner, *Stone Fox* (courage, perseverance)

Kirkpatrick Hill, *Toughboy and Sister* (survival, Aboriginal)

James Houston, *Tikta'Liktak* (Inuit, survival)

Glenn McCoy, *The Legend of Spud Murphy* (librarian, fantasy)

Ellen Miles, *Taylor Made Tales: The Dog's Secret*

Alexander McCall Smith, *Akimbo and the Lions* (Africa, boy and cub)

Jerry Spinelli, *Fourth Grade Rats* (conformity, peers)

Jeanne Willis, *Dumb Creatures* (elective mute connects with gorilla)

Grade 5

Marion Dane Bauer, *Runt: Story of a Boy* (poverty, abuse, friendship, courage)

Mary Chase, *The Wicked Wicked Ladies in the Haunted House*

Andrew Clements, *The Report Card* (gifted, trying to fit in)

Sandy Frances Duncan, *Cariboo Runaway* (historical, goldrush)

Elin Kelsey, *Strange New Species* (invitation to pursue research)

Dick King Smith, *Just Binnie* (WWI, Edwardian, family)

Sofia Nordin, *In the Wild* (adventure, survival, bullying)

Jerry Spinelli, *Wringer* (facing fears, courage, tradition)

Cora Taylor, *Ghost Voyage (I, II, III)* (Canadian explorers)

Wendelin Van Draanen, *Shredderman Series* (creative way of dealing with bullies)

Grades 5–6

Blue Balliett, *Chasing Vermeer* (art, math, mystery)

Frank Cottell Boyce, *Millions* (greed, decisions, character develop-siblings

Zizou Corder, *Lion Boy* (boy communicates with cats, uncovers parents' kidnapping)

Jonathan Harlen, *The Cockroach War* (siblings win lottery)

Kathryn Lansky, *The Night Journey* (WWII, Jewish persecution)

Gary Paulson, *The Hatchet* (survival, adventure)

Jerry Spinelli, *Loser*

Theodore Taylor, *Ice Drift* (Arctic, ice fishing, survival)

Grade 6

Deborah Ellis, *The Breadwinner* (Afghanistan, freedom, culture)

Frances Mary Hendry, *Chandra* (South Asian culture, traditions)

Eva Ibbotson, *Journey to the River Sea* (adventure, Amazon River)

Eva Ibbotson, *The Star of Kazan* (1900 Vienna, old-fashioned adventure)

Cynthia Kadohata, *Weedflowers* (WWII, Pearl Harbor)

Ben Mikaelsen, *Petey* (friendship, overcoming physical obstacles, discrimination)

Kenneth Oppel, *Silverwing* (bat colony, survival)

Linda Sue Park, *A Single Chard* (Korea, 12th century)

Michelle Paver, *Wolf Brother* (first in "Chronicles of Ancient Darkness" series set in Bronze Age, friendship between boy and wolf cub, survival, adventure, loyalty)

Christopher Russell, *Brind and the Dogs of War* (boy raised by dogs)

Lois Sachar, *Holes* (crime and punishment, consequences)

Lois Sachar, *Small Steps* (sequel to Holes)

Jonathan Stroud, *Buried Fire* (fantasy, dragons, secrets, choices)

Tim Wynne-Jones, *The Maestro* (coming of age, friendship, courage, piano)

Grade 7

Peter Abrahams, *Down the Rabbit Hole* (girl protagonist, sports, drama, mystery)

Terry Deary, *The Fire Thief* (adaptation of Greek myth)

Deborah Ellis, *Looking for X* (loyalty, bullying, autism, family; easy, short read, occasional coarse language)

Margaret Peterson Haddix, *The House on the Gulf* (thriller, mystery)

Carl Hiaasen, *Hoot* (owls, environment, bullying)

Elizabeth Laird, *The Garbage King* (third-world poverty, deprivation, survival)

Caroline Laurence, *Roman Mystery Series* (mystery in Ancient Rome)

Jean Little, *Willow and Twig* (abandonment, drug addiction, survival)

Ben Mikaelsen, *Touching Spirit Bear* (Aboriginal, survival, self-realization)

Michael Morpurgo, *Private Peaceful* (WW I)

Alex Shearer. *Tins* (boy collects tin cans, finds body parts)

Jerry Spinelli, *Star Girl* (acceptance, nonconformity, peers, loyalty)

Maiya Williams, *The Golden Hour* (time travel, French Revolution)

Paul Yee, *The Bone Collector's Son* (1907 Vancouver, ghosts)

Avi, *Crispin: The Cross of Lead* (medieval England, boy accused of crime he didn't commit, survival, adventure)

Ann Halam, *Dr. Franklin's Island* (plane crash, survival)

Mary Hooper, *At the Sign of the Sugared Plum* (plague, 17th-century London)

Michael Morpurgo, *War Horse* and *Farm Boy* (two books: same story, different points of view)

Wendelin Van Draanen, *Flipped* (early teen relationship/romance)

Pam Withers, *Raging River* (adventure, survival, extreme sports)

Reading Power and Parents

Reading at home with your child has long been regarded as one of the most important things a parent can do to assist in their child's learning. In my experience, most parents, when reading at home with their beginning reader, do what many of us in the teaching profession have been guilty of: they concentrate on the code, on the "saying of the words," and often forget about the comprehension. "Learning to read," in the eyes of many parents, is "learning to say the words on the page." Introducing parents to Reading Power—the concepts of strategic thinking, making meaning, metacognition, and the language of thinking—will help guide their support away from a focus on decoding towards a balance with understanding.

I believe parents have the best intentions when reading at home with their children, but they may not know how to move beyond helping their child say the words on the page. Parents I have worked with over the years are eager to know how they can help their children—they just need to be shown how. Providing a simple strategy with simple language that they can at home gives them the practical tools to help their child read.

During the years that I have taught Reading Power, I have been invited to many parent nights, PAC meetings, and Family Literacy celebrations. I show up with my Reading Power poster and a tub of books, and proceed to give parents a brief overview of the research and the concept of metacognition, explaining each strategy. I then model, with a picture book, what reading at home with their child might look like and sound like, using the Reading Power strategies and language. The response has been extremely positive; parents enjoy sharing their connections and experiences with one another. They leave, grateful for a new strategy and eager to try it at home with their child. Many have told me afterwards how much more they enjoy reading with their children and how much their children enjoy hearing their parents' "stories."

If you are planning a Parent Information Session, here are some guidelines:

- One or two teachers present a brief overview of Reading Power. They demonstrate the concept of metacognition using the Reading Powers Model (page 20).
- Choose one strategy to model; Connecting is a good one to start with.
- A teacher models the Speaking voice/Thinking voice read-aloud with a book, using the phrase "This reminds me of…."
- Have a collection of Connect books spread out on a table. Invite parents to choose one and read quietly to themselves, paying attention to their connections.
- Parents partner to share their books and their connections.

I encourage parents who do not speak English at home to practise these strategies in their own language.

- If the parents are there during school time, invite their children to leave class and join their parents. Have parent and child read together and share their connections.
- Pass out the parent information sheet (pages 123–124) and Parent Information Bookmark (page 125) to take home. If possible, provide a resource list of Connect books.
- The Reading Power Overview (page 126) could be used in a fall school newsletter or in the first-term report-card overview.

Reading Power

Helping Your Children Become
More Powerful Readers and Thinkers

A Guide for Parents

"Meaning is constructed in the realm where readers meet the words in the text and consider the ideas in terms of their own experience and knowledge."

—Stephanie Harvey

What is Reading Power?

Reading Power is a reading comprehension program that teachers at this school are using to help students develop comprehension skills to become more powerful readers and thinkers. The five comprehension strategies, or Reading Powers, we are teaching are:

1. **Connect:** What does the story remind me of?

2. **Question:** What am I wondering about this story?

3. **Visualize:** What pictures can I make in my head from this story?

4. **Infer:** What am I thinking about this story that isn't actually written?

5. **Transform:** How has my thinking changed because of this story?

What are the Key Ideas?

- Learning to read involves two distinct, yet equally important components:
  Decoding: the ability to read the words on the page with fluency and accuracy
  Comprehension: the ability to construct meaning from the text

- Comprehension strategies need to be **taught directly** and explicitly so that students can understand what thinking looks like and sounds like.

- **Common language** of these thinking strategies is essential for helping students acquire the "language of thinking" across the grades.

- **Metacognition**, or "awareness of thinking," is an important component of this program

- We have two voices: a **speaking voice** and a **thinking voice**. Good readers pay attention to their **thinking voice** while they read.

- Teachers and parents can **model** their **thinking voice** while they read to and with their children, to help teach and reinforce the strategies

---

Connecting

"Your life is a story —it's just not written down on paper"

What is it?

Powerful readers make **connections** with what they are reading. When we read a story, it may **remind** each of us of different things. This **reminding** is also called **"connecting."** We can make connections to personal experiences, other books, other media like movies, or experiences in the world.

How to Connect with your children:

- Choose a book to read with your child that evokes memories for you: memories of your childhood, your family, your culture, your school days, your country, etc.

- Begin to read the book out loud with your "speaking voice."

- Whenever something in the story reminds you of a personal experience, stop reading and share your connection: "This part of the story reminds me of…"

- Continue reading the story with your "speaking voice" and sharing your connections, or your "thinking voice."

- Ask your child to share any connections she or he might have.

- It is important to remember that, just as everyone's life story—memories and personal experiences—is different, connections are also different. There is no right or wrong way to make a connection.

Enjoy reading and sharing connections and with your child!

Parent Information Bookmark

Front of bookmark

Back of bookmark

Reading Power Connecting

Reading Power Connecting

When we read a story, it reminds each of us of different things. This reminding is also called "connecting."

It reminds me of…

My memories.

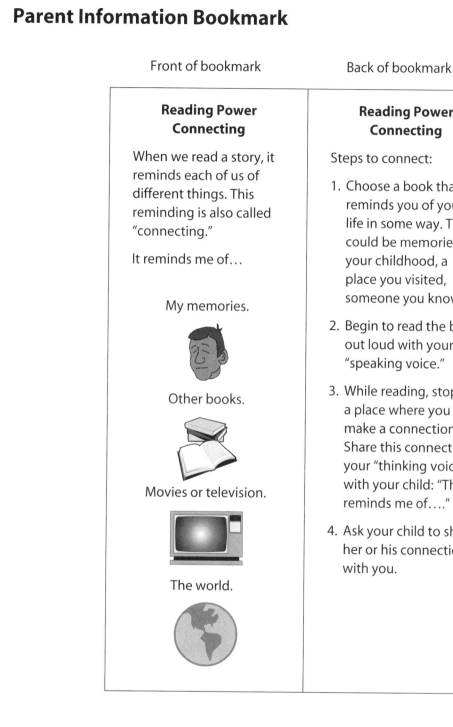

Other books.

Movies or television.

The world.

Steps to connect:

1. Choose a book that reminds you of your life in some way. This could be memories of your childhood, a place you visited, someone you know.

2. Begin to read the book out loud with your "speaking voice."

3. While reading, stop at a place where you make a connection. Share this connection, your "thinking voice," with your child: "This reminds me of…."

4. Ask your child to share her or his connections with you.

Reading Power: An Overview

Reading Power is a research-based reading comprehension program currently being implemented into our school. Our goal in reading is not only to teach students how to become fluent decoders, but also to teach students to develop an awareness of their thinking while they read, so that they can engage in a deeper, more meaningful reading experiences and improve their comprehension. Using authentic children's literature, students are introduced to five specific during-reading strategies, or Reading Powers, that have been found, in research, to be ones used by proficient readers. The five reading powers are: CONNECT, QUESTION, VISUALIZE, INFER, and TRANSFORM. Students will be spending class time learning and practising these Reading Powers, and will be taught how each one can help to enhance their understanding of what they read. Related writing extensions will also be integrated into the program.

CONNECT: the ability to make connections between the story you are reading and your own life experiences.

QUESTION: the ability to ask both literal and deep-thinking questions while you read

VISUALIZE: the ability to use the words in a text to create mental images, or a "movie in your mind" while you read.

INFER: the ability to look for clues within the text and pictures while you read and to use these clues to "fill in" what is not written directly in the text.

TRANSFORM: the understanding that books have the capability of transforming (changing) the way you view yourself, others, and the world; the ability to identify the things in a book that matter most to you.

Assessment

"Assessment is descriptive information about learning."
—Faye Brownlie, *Grand Conversations, Thoughtful Responses*

Assessment needs to be reflective of our goals. If our goal as teachers is that our students be able to read a passage and correctly answer a series of comprehension questions, then our assessment needs to reflect that. Many traditional assessments of reading comprehension do just that: provide students with passages to read and questions to be answered. And while valuable information about our students' comprehension can be gained from these formal assessment tools, I believe it is also important for teachers to look beyond whether or not a student is "getting the right answer," to try to evaluate *how* they are getting those answers. There is a need, therefore, to reassess our reading goals for our students in order to better assess their comprehension skills and help guide our practice.

Goals of Reading Comprehension

As a teacher of reading, my goals for my students are that they

- develop an awareness of thinking; become metacognitive learners
- develop a language of thinking to articulate their understanding of the text
- identify and use specific thinking strategies, enabling them to make meaning from the text
- understand how and why specific strategies can be used to deepen their understanding of the text

ASSESSING THE GOALS

The Reading Power Questionnaire (page 128) will help assess the first goal—have the students developed an awareness of their thinking, or become metacognitive learners? I like to give this questionnaire early in September to assess where my students are in their understanding of thinking. If it is your first year teaching Reading Power, you will likely find that many of your students are not familiar with the strategies; if your school has already implemented this common language of comprehension, the students you receive in the fall will already have been exposed to some of the strategies. The questionnaire will provide you with insight to guide your teaching, and will help you establish which strategies you may need to focus on. For example, if most of your class is regularly making connections, then you may not need to be spending as much time on the Connect strategy. Towards the end of the school year, I give the class the same questionnaire and then compare each individual's results to see where growth has taken place.

Reading Power Questionnaire

Name: _____   Date: _____

Grade: _____

1. What parts of the body do you use when you read?

_____

_____

2. What things did you need to learn in order for you to be able to read?
(E.g., "I need to know the alphabet ")

_____

_____

Circle the best answer for you:

1. When I read, I make connections between what I am reading and my own experiences, other books, and the world around me.

    Always   Often   Sometimes   Never

2. While I'm reading, I ask myself questions about the story.

    Always   Often   Sometimes   Never

3. While I'm reading, I make pictures in my head about what is happening in the story.

    Always   Often   Sometimes   Never

(For students above Grade 1)

4. While I'm reading, I fill in words or pictures in my head that the author didn't include.

    Always   Often   Sometimes   Never

5. While I'm reading, my ideas, thoughts, and opinions about what I'm reading will change.

    Always   Often   Sometimes   Never

INFORMAL ASSESSMENT

Informal evaluation provides us with invaluable insight into our student progress. The Reading Power Checklist on page 130, created by a teacher in Richmond, is an informal list that you can keep close by during direct and guided lessons. When you begin to recognize students who are demonstrating an understanding of a particular strategy, you can jot down quick comments or check beside their names. Similarly, if you see that a student is struggling to understand a strategy, a quick note beside the student's name will remind you that this child may need extra support.

FORMAL ASSESSMENT

When you want to go deeper into individual's understanding of each of the Reading Powers, the Comprehension Assessment on page 131 can be used. This can be used as an individual interview with each student after a strategy is taught, or as a whole-class assessment. In the case of a whole class-assessment, you may want to choose one story to read aloud and then have the students write their responses. For primary students, you may need to read the questions aloud and leave time in between for students to write their responses.

This form may be used for ongoing assessment, where students fill out only the portion of the sheet pertaining to the most recently taught strategy. Or, for students familiar with all the strategies, it can be given periodically throughout the year. Noticing the gaps in the students' understanding of certain strategies will help to guide your practice and show you which Reading Powers may require more teaching.

The Reading Power Rubric on pages 132–133 outlines, on a five-point scale, the range from Exceeding to Not Yet Meeting levels of demonstration, understanding, and output for each of the five Reading Powers. These are not provincial performance standards, but were created as some common standards for assessing and reporting these five comprehension strategies.

Reading Power Checklist

Name: _____

Date: _____

Student Name	Connect		Question		Visualize		Infer		Transform

Comprehension Assessment

Student Name: _____   Grade: _____   Div: _____

Title: _____

Reading Power	Question	Student Response
Connect	Can you tell me what connecting is? Can you tell me some different ways you can make a connection (i.e. T–S,T–T, T–W, T–feeling, T–character)? Give me an example of a connection you made to this story.	
Question	Can you tell me the difference between a quick question and a deep-thinking question? Give me an example of each from this story and then try to answer them.	
Visualize	Can you tell me what visualizing is? Can you tell me about a part in this story where you visualized? What words helped you? Tell me about some other senses you used besides what you saw.	
Infer	Can you tell me what inferring is? What are you doing when you infer? What things help you to infer? Give me an example of inferring from this story. Give me a "maybe" thought that you had on this page.	
Transform	Can you tell me what transforming is? When does thinking change when you are reading? Give me an example of how your thinking changed when you read this story.	

Reading Power Rubric

	Exceeds	Fully Meets	Meets	Minimally Meets	Not Yet Meeting
CONNECT	• fully understands the strategy of connecting to text and how to use these personal connections cognitively, orally, and in written form to enhance understanding of what he/she is reading • connects to self (T–S), other texts (T–T), and the world (T–W) without prompting	• understands the strategy of connecting to text, and is easily able to make personal connections to the stories he/she is reading to enhance his/her understanding • connects to self (T–S), other texts (T–T), and the world (T–W) with prompting	• is learning how to make personal connections with the text he/she is reading in order to make better sense of the story; can express simple connections orally and in written form with no prompting • makes connections that are relevant and enhance comprehension	• has been introduced to the during-reading strategy of connecting to text, and is beginning to understand how connections can help enhance understanding of the story; can make a connection when prompted, but it is not always meaningful to the story • makes connections that may be more literal than inferential	• is not yet able to make (or requires support when making) personal connections to stories he/she is reading in order to better understand the text
QUESTION	• is able to ask him/herself thoughtful questions, both literal and deep-thinking, during the reading process, and understands fully how these questions, answered or not, can lead to a greater understanding of the text	• is able to ask thoughtful questions during the reading process, and understands how the process of asking and answering questions while reading can help him/her better understand the text; evidence of both literal and inferential (deep-thinking) questioning is present	• is learning the strategy of asking him/herself questions while reading, and is demonstrating a beginning understanding of how the answers to these questions can help enhance understanding of the text; questions are generally literal with some evidence of inferential	• is learning to ask him/herself simple questions about the story he/she is reading, and demonstrates minimal understanding of how this strategy can be used to enhance comprehension of the text	• is not yet able to ask him/herself questions about a text while reading, nor to demonstrate an understanding of how this reading strategy may help him/her understand the text better
VISUALIZE	• can easily and naturally combine the words in a text with his/her own background knowledge to create mental images while reading, as demonstrated in both oral, written and drawn responses • is easily able to incorporate the senses to mental images • fully understands that visualizing while reading will help to enhance comprehension and bring reading to life	• is able to use the words in a text to create mental images while reading, demonstrates this in both written and drawn responses • incorporates some of the senses to mental images • fully understands how visualizing while reading can help to enhance understanding of the text	• is learning to use the words in a text to create mental images while reading, and is attempting to use this strategy while reading independently, as demonstrated by oral, written, and drawn responses • attempts to incorporate more than one sense when visualizing	• is beginning to use the words in a text to create a "movie in the mind" while reading, and demonstrates a beginning understanding of this strategy as demonstrated in oral and drawn responses • is not yet able to utilize more than one sense in unless prompted	• is not demonstrating competence or understanding of visualizing (creating mental images of what is happening in a story while reading) unless there are pictures or illustrations to support him/her

Reading Power Rubric (continued)

	Exceeds	Fully Meets	Meets	Minimally Meets	Not Yet Meeting
INFER	• demonstrates complete understanding of the difference between a fact and an inference. While reading, is competent in looking for clues within the text and pictures, and combines these clues with his/her own background knowledge to help "fill in" and interpret the text	• understands the difference between a fact (something that is written explicitly in the text) and an inference (something that is implied within the text); while reading, is able to look for clues in text and in pictures and is learning to infer meaning from them by responding with "I think …" or Maybe …"	• is beginning to demonstrate an understanding of the difference between a fact and an inference, and is learning how to look for clues in both pictures and text that will help him/her to make these inferences and make better sense of the text	• demonstrates a beginning understanding of what an inference is and, with support, is learning to look for clues within the text and pictures to help him/her make these inferences	• has difficulty distinguishing the difference between a fact (something written explicitly in the text) and an inference (something the reader interprets based on clues within the text) and is not yet able to make inferences independently while reading
TRANSFORM	• understands fully that books have the ability to change the way we think about ourselves and our world, and is able to look beyond the pages of the text towards the implications and affects the book may have on his/her own life as demonstrated in written and oral responses	• understands that books have the ability to change the way we think about ourselves and our world, and is able to look for and identify things in a book that matter most to him/her as demonstrated in written responses	• is learning that a story has the power to change the way we think about ourselves, others, and the world around us. and is learning to identify things in a book that matter most to him/her	• is demonstrating minimal understanding of what it means to be transformed by a book and, with teacher support, is learning to identify important issues in books that may change the way he/she thinks	• is not yet demonstrating an understanding of Transform, and is unable to identify important issues in books which may change the way one might view themselves or the world

Final Thoughts

"Making a difference means making it different."
—Dame Marie Clay

Since its early stages several years ago, I have known in my heart that there was something about Reading Power that made it unique, something about it that was different from other teaching methods or reading programs I had tried. First and foremost, it has helped to fill in for me the missing piece of teaching reading—that in order for us to help our students become better readers, we need to teach them how to become better thinkers. I believe the power of Reading Power is that it teaches students not what to think, but how to think.

If our goal is teaching students to learn how to think, then we, as their teachers, need to make a strong commitment to achieving that goal:

- considering ourselves "teachers of reading" no matter what grade we teach
- integrating metacognition into our teaching practice to help students become aware of their thinking
- increasing our instructional time teaching students comprehension strategies
- building a common language of reading and thinking across the grades and integrating the language of thinking intentionally into our classrooms, so that students can build on their knowledge of reading and thinking as they progress through their school years
- modeling and demonstrating our thinking voices to students, so that they see what thinking looks like and sounds like
- filling classrooms with rich, thought-provoking literature, and being passionate about the books we share with our students
- helping students believe that they have the "power" to become good readers.

Reading Power enables students to take control of their own reading, invites them to think their own thoughts beyond the pages of the book, and encourages them to open their eyes, their minds, and their hearts to the power of believing that their thoughts matter.

What else makes Reading Power unique? Madeline Silva, an extraordinary Grade 3 teacher, said to me one day that the reason she loved teaching Reading Power so much was that it was "respectful of children's thoughts." Reading Power respects children's thinking by teaching them that their thoughts, their connections, their images, their questions, and their insights are the most important things when it comes to constructing meaning.

Dame Marie Clay, when speaking of her Reading Recovery program for struggling readers, stated, "Making a difference means making it different." I see a parallel here to Reading Power. If we want to make a difference in our students' ability to comprehend text, we need to make our teaching different. By teaching students that reading is not just words on a page, but what of ourselves and of our thinking we can bring to those words, and by providing them with a common language to use to think and talk about reading, then I believe we truly can "make a difference." To read is to think—to think is to become. Nothing we teach our children in school could be more powerful.

Bibliography

Professional Resources

Albom, Mitch (2003) *The Five People You Meet in Heaven*. New York, NY: Hyperion.

Anderson, R.C. & P.D. Pearson (1984) "A Schema-Theoretic View of Basic Process in Reading." In *Handbook of Reading Research*, ed. P.D. Pearson. White Plains, NY: Longman.

Brownlie, Faye (2005) *Grand Conversations, Thoughtful Responses: A Unique Approach to Literature Circles*. Winnipeg, MN: Portage and Main Press.

Charlton, James (1991) *The Writer's Quotation Book: A Literary Companion*. New York, NY: Viking.

Dillard, Annie (1989) *The Writing Life*. New York, NY: HarperCollins.

Fielding, Linda & Pearson, David P. (1994) "Reading Comprehension: What Works?" *Educational Leadership 51*, 5:62-67.

Gilbar, Steve (1990) *The Readers Quotation Book*. New York, NY: Viking.

Graves, Donald (1991) *Building a Literate Classroom*. New York, NY: Irwin.

Hall, Susan (1990) *Using Picture Storybooks to Teach Literary Devices*. Phoenix, AZ: Oryx Press.

Harwayne, Shelley (1992) *Lasting Impressions: Weaving Literature into the Writing Workshop*. Portsmouth, NH: Heinemann.

Harvey, Stephanie (1998) *Nonfiction Matters: Reading, Writing, and Research in Grades 3–8*. Portland, ME: Stenhouse.

Harvey, Stephanie & Goudvis, Anne (2000) *Strategies That Work: Teaching Comprehension to Enhance Understanding*. Portland, ME: Stenhouse.

Johnston, Peter H. (2004) *Choice Words: How Our Language Affects Children's Learning*. Portland, ME: Stenhouse.

Lamont, Anne (1994) *Bird by Bird: Some Instructions on Writing and Life*. New York, NY: Anchor Books.

McCourt, Frank (2005) *Teacher Man*. New York, NY: Charles Scribner.

Michaels, Anne (1996) *Fugitive Pieces*. Toronto, ON: McClelland & Stewart.

Miller, Debbie (2002) *Reading with Meaning: Teaching comprehension in the primary grades*. Portland, ME: Stenhouse.

Morrison, Toni (2006) "The Reader as Artist" *Oprah Magazine*, Volume 7, Number 7.

Proulx, Annie (1993) *The Shipping News*. New York, NY: Charles Scribner.

Quindlen, Anna (1998) *How Reading Changed My Life*. New York, NY: Ballantine Books.

Routman, R. (2003) *Reading Essentials: The Specifics You Need to Teach Reading Well*. Portsmouth, NH: Heinemann.

Wilkinson, Mary Ruth K. (2000) *A Time to Read: Good Books for Growing Readers*. Vancouver, BC: Regent College Publishing.

Zimmerman, Susan & Keene, Ellin Oliver (1997) *Mosaic of Thought*. Portsmouth, NH: Heinemann.

Children's Books

Abercrombie, Barbara. *Charlie Anderson*. McElderry Books, 1990.

Abrahams, Peter. *Down the Rabbit Hole*. HarperCollins, 2005.

Adams, Dawn. *The Forest*. Queen Charlotte Island Reader. Pacific Educational Press.

Alborough, Jez. *Hug*. Candlewick, 2002.

—*Watch Out, Big Bro's Coming*! Candlewick, 1997.

Alderson, Sue Ann. *Ida and the Wool Smugglers*. Douglas & McIntyre, 1999.

Aliki. *Painted Words/Spoken Memories: Marianthe's Story*. Greenwillow, 1998.

—*The Two of Them*. HarperCollins, 1978.

Allard, Harry G. *Miss Nelson Is Missing*. Houghton Mifflin, 1997.

Anholt, Catherine & Laurence. *Good Days, Bad Days*. Raincoast, 1991.

—*What Makes Me Happy*. Candlewick, 2002.

Asch, Frank. *Water*. Harcourt, 2001

Ashley, Bernard. *Cleversticks*. Crown Books for Young Readers, 1992.

Austin, Margot. *A Friend for Growl Bear*. HarperCollins, 1999.

Avi. *Crispin: The Cross of Lead*. Hyperion, 2004.

Baker, Jeannie. *Where the Forest Meets the Sea*. William Morrow, 1987.

Baker, Keith. *Little Green*. Harcourt, 2001.

—*Who Is the Beast?* Harcourt, 2001.

Balliett, Blue. *Chasing Vermeer*. Scholastic, 2004.

Bang, Molly. *When Sophie Gets Angry — Really, Really Angry*. Scholastic Canada, 1999.

Banks, Lynne Reid. *Harry the Poisonous Centipede*. HarperCollins, 1996.

Bauer, Marion Dane. *Runt: Story of a Boy*. Milkweed Editions, 2006.

Baylor, Bird. *Guess Who My Favorite Person Is*. Charles Scribner, 1986.

— *The Table Where Rich People Sit*. Aladdin, 1994.

Beaumont, Karen. *I Like Myself*. Harcourt, 2004.

Below, Halina. *The Windy Day*. Lester, 1994.

Berger, Barbara. *Grandfather Twilight*. Putnam, 1984.

Best, Cari. *Goose's Story*. Farrar, Straus & Giroux, 2002.

— *Shrinking Violet*. NY: Farrar, Straus & Giroux, 2001.

Bisson, Pat. *The Summer My Father Was Ten*. Boyds Mills, 1998.

Bloom, Suzanne. *A Splendid Friend, Indeed*. Scholastic, 2005.

Blume, Judy. *The Pain and the Great One*. Simon & Schuster, 1984

Blumenthal, Diana Cain. *I'm Not Invited*. Simon & Schuster, 2003.

Boelts, Maribeth. *When It's the Last Day of School*. Putnam, 2004.

Bogart, Jo Ellen. *The Night the Stars Flew*. Northwinds, 2001.

Booth, David. *Voices in the Wind: Poems for All Seasons*. Kids Can Press, 1990.

Borden, Louise. *The Day Eddie Met the Author*. Simon & Schuster, 2001.

Bottner, Barbara. *Bootsie Barker Bites*. Putnam, 2002.

Bourgeois, Paulette. *Franklin Is Bossy*. Kids Can Press, 1993.

— *Franklin Plays the Game*. Kids Can Press, 1995.

— *Franklin's Bad Day*. Kids Can Press, 1996.

— *Franklin's New Friend*. Kids Can Press, 1997.

— *Franklin's Secret Club*. Kids Can Press, 1998.

Boyce, Frank Cotrell. *Millions*. Macmillan, 2004.

Brett, Jan. *The Umbrella*. PYRG, 2004.

Brown, Margaret Wise. *The Big Red Barn*. HarperCollins, 1987

— *The Color Kittens*. Golden Books, 1986.

— *The Sailor Dog*.: Golden Books, 1981.

Browne, Anthony. (1990). *Changes*. Knopf, 1990.

— *Into the Forest*. Candlewick, 2004.

— *The Piggybook*. Dragonfly Books, 1989.

— *The Shape Game*. Transworld Distribution, 1989.

— *Things I Like*. Knopf, 1989.

— *Voices in the Park*. Dorling Kindersley, 1998.

— *Willy and Hugh*. Douglas & McIntyre, 1991.

— *Willy the Champ*. Candlewick, 1983.

— *Willy the Dreamer*. Walker Books, 2000.

— *Willy the Wimp*. Knopf, 1984.

— *Willy the Wizard*. Douglas & McIntyre, 1995

— *Zoo*. Farrar, Straus & Giroux, 1992.

Bruchac, Joseph. *A Boy Called Slow*. Puffin, 2002.

— *Fox Song*. Putnam, 1997.

Brumbeau, Jeff. *The Quilt Maker's Gift*. Scholastic, 2000.

Bunting, Eve. (1991). *Fly Away Home*. Clarion, 1991.

— *Gleam and Glow*. Clarion, 2000.

— *Riding the Tiger*. Houghton Mifflin, 2001.

— *The Memory String*. Clarion, 2000.

— *The Sunflower House*. Clarion, 1989.

— *The Wednesday Surprise*. Clarion, 1989.

Burningham, John. *Aldo*. Crown Books for Young Readers, 1992.

— *Come Away From the Water, Shirley!* HarperCollins, 1977.

— *Hey! (Oi!) Get Off Our Train!* Random House, 1989.

— *Seasons*. Random House, 1993.

— *Time to Get Out of the Bath, Shirley!* HarperCollins, 1978.

Cain, Janan. *The Way I Feel*. Parenting Press, 2000.

Carlson, Nancy. *I Like Me!* Puffin, 1988.

— *Loudmouth George and the Sixth-Grade Bully*. Puffin, 1985.

— *There's a Big Beautiful World Out There!* Penguin, 2002

Carman, William. *What's that Noise?* Random House, 2002.

Carr, Jan. *Splish, Splash, Spring!* Holiday House, 2001.

Carrier, Roch. *The Hockey Sweater*. Tundra, 1979.

Carroll, Lewis. *Jabberwocky*. Albert Whitman, 1985.

Castle, Caroline. *For Every Child: The UN Convention on the Rights of the Child.* Dial, 2001.

Cave, Kathryn. *That's What Friends Do.* Hyperion, 2004.

Champion, Joyce. *Emily and Alice, Best Friends.* Harcourt, 1993.

Chase, Edith Newlin. *Secret Dawn.* Firefly, 1996.

— *Waters.* Firefly, 1993.

Chase, Mary. *The Wicked Wicked Ladies in the Haunted House.* Dell Yearling, 1968.

Cherry, Lynn. *The Great Kapok Tree.* Harcourt Brace, 1990.

Chinn, Karen. *Sam and the Lucky Money.* Lee & Low, 1995.

Chodos-Irvine, Margaret. *Ella Sarah Gets Dressed.* Harcourt, 2003.

Christiansen, Candace. *The Mitten Tree.* Putnam, 1995.

Churchill, Vicki. *Sometimes I Like to Curl Up in a Ball.* Sterling Publishing, 2001.

Clements, Andrew. *The Report Card.* Aladdin, 2004.

Coerr, Eleanor. *Sadako.* Putman, 1977.

Condra, Estelle. *See the Ocean.* Ideal Children's Books, 1994.

Cooney, Barbara. *Miss Rumphius.* Viking Penguin, 1982.

Corder, Zizou. *Lion Boy.* Puffin, 2003.

Costanzo, Charlene. (1999). *The Twelve Gifts of Birth.* HarperCollins, 1999.

Coville, Bruce. *The Prince of Butterflies.* Harcourt, 2002.

Cox, Phil Roxbee. *Don't Be a Bully, Billy!* Usborne, 2004.

— *Give That Back, Jack!* Usborne, 2004.

Coy, John. *Night Driving.* Henry Holt, 1996.

Crow, Allan. *The Crying Christmas Tree.* Pemmican, 2001.

Crum, Shutta. *Click!* Fitzhenry & Whiteside, 2003.

Cumming, Peter. *Out on the Ice in the Middle of the Bay.* Annick, 1993.

Curtis, Jamie Lee. *When I Was Little: A Four Year Old's Memoir of Her Youth.* Scholastic, 1993.

Cutler, Jane. *The Cello of Mr. O.* Penguin, 1999.

Dabcovich, Lydia. *The Polar Bear Son.* Clarion, 1997.

Dahl, Roald. *Charlie and the Chocolate Factory.* Knopf Canada, 1964.

Day, Alexandra. *Carl Goes Shopping.* Farrar, Straus & Giroux, 1989.

— *Good Dog Carl.* Simon & Schuster, 1985.

Deary, Terry. *The Fire Thief.* Kingfisher, 2005.

Demers, Dominique. *Every Single Night.* Groundwood, 2006.

— *Old Thomas and the Little Fairy.* Dominique & Friends, 2000.

Dene Children of La Loche and Friends. *Byron Through the Seasons: A Dene-English Story Book. (Byron Bel Haet'aziluke sine.)* Fifth House Publishers, 1999.

DePaola, Tomie. *The Art Lesson.* Putman, 1989.

— *Nana Upstairs, Nana Downstairs.* Puffin, 1978.

— *Oliver Button Is a Sissy.* Harcourt Brace, 1979.

— *Pancakes for Breakfast.* Harcourt Brace, 2001.

Downey, Roma. *Love Is a Family.* ReganBooks, 2001.

Drucker, Malka. *Grandma's Latkes.* Harcourt Brace, 1996.

Duksta, Laura. *I Love You More.* I Shine, 2001.

Dunbar, Joyce. *The Sand Children.* Crocodile Books, 1999.

Duncan, Sandy Frances. *Cariboo Runaway.* Pacific Edge, 1997.

Edwards, Becky. *My Brother Sammy.* Bloomsbury, 1999.

— *My Cat Charlie.* Bloomsbury, 2001.

Edwards, Pamela Duncan. *Some Smug Slug.* HarperCollins, 1996.

Ehlert, Lois. *Top Cat.* Harcourt, 2001.

Einarson, Earl. *The Moccasins.* Theytus Books, 1994.

Ellis, Deborah. *The Breadwinner.* Groundwood, 2000.

— *Looking for X.* Groundwood, 1999.

— *Parvana's Journey.* Groundwood, 2002.

Elvgren, Jennifer Riesmeyer. *Josias, Hold the Book.* Boyd Mills Press, 2006.

Erdrich, Louise. *Grandmother's Pigeon.* Hyperion, 1999.

Ering, Timothy Basil. *The Story of Frog Belly Rat Bone.* Penguin, 2003.

Ets, Marie Hall. *Gilberto and the Wind.* Puffin, 1978.

Evyindson, Peter. *Jen and the Great One.* Pemmican, 1990.

— *Red Parka Mary.* Pemmican, 1995.

Falconer, Ian. *Olivia.* Atheneum, 2000.

Feiffer, Jules. *I Lost My Bear.* HarperCollins, 1998.

— *Meanwhile.* HarperCollins, 1997.

Fernandes, Eugenie. *A Difficult Day.* Kids Can Press, 1999.

— *Waves in the Bathtub.* Kids Can Press, 1993.

Fienberg, Anne. *Horrendo's Curse.* Annick, 2002.

Fienburg, Barbara. *Tashi.* Allen & Unwin, 1995.

Fitch, Sheree. *No Two Snowflakes.* Orca , 2001.

Fitzpatrick, Marie-Louise. *The Long March: The Choctaw's Gift to Irish Famine Relief.* Beyond Words Publishing, 1998.

Fleischman, Paul. *Rondo in C.* HarperCollins, 1988.

— *The Sidewalk Circus.* Candlewick, 2004.

— *Weslandia.* Candlewick, 1999.

Fleming, Denise. *In the Small, Small Pond.* Scholastic, 1993.

— *In the Tall, Tall Grass.* Henry Holt, 1991.

— *Where Once There Was a Wood.* Henry Holt, 1996.

Fox, Mem. *Feathers and Fools.* Harcourt, 1998.

— *Tough Boris.* Harcourt, 2001.

— *Wilfred Gordon Macdonald Partridge.* Kane/Miller Books, 1989.

— *Whoever You Are.* Harcourt, 2001.

Fraser, Mary Ann. *I.Q. Goes to School.* Walker & Co, 2002.

Frasier, Debra. *Out of the Ocean.* Harcourt, 2001.

Gammell, Stephen. *Ride.* Harcourt, 2001.

Gardiner, John Reynolds. *Stone Fox.* Trophy, 1980.

Gardiner, Lindsey. *Not Fair, Won't Share!* Barrons, 2001.

Garland, Sherry. *The Lotus Seed.* Harcourt Brace, 1993.

Gay, Marie-Louise. *Mademoiselle Moon.* Groundwood, 1996.

— *Stella, Fairy of the Forest.* Vancouver Art Gallery, 2002.

— *Stella, Queen of the Snow.* Groundwood, 2002.

— *Stella, Star of the Sea.* Groundwood, 2004.

Gerber, Mary J. *Thanks for Thanksgiving.* Scholastic, 1998.

Gilliland, Judith Heide. *Not in the House, Newton.* Clarion, 1995.

Gilmor, Don. *When Vegetables Go Bad.* Doubleday, 1994.

Gilmore, Rachna. *A Screaming Kind of Day*. Fitzhenry & Whiteside, 1999.

Gliori, Debi. *My Little Brother*. Candlewick, 1995.

Godwin, Patricia. *I Feel Orange Today*. Annick, 1993.

Goldin, Barbara Diamond. *The Girl Who Lived with the Bears*. Harcourt Brace, 1997.

Haddix, Margaret Peterson. *The House on the Gulf*. Aladdin, 2004.

Halam, Ann. *Dr. Franklin's Island*. Laurel-Leaf Books, 2003.

Hamanaka, Sheila. *All the Colors of the Earth*. William Morrow, 1994.

Harlen, Jonathan. *The Cockroach War*. Allen & Unwin, 2003.

Harper, Charise Mericle. *The Invisible Mistakecase*. Houghton Mifflin, 2005.

Harris, Dorothy Joan. *A Very Unusual Dog*. Scholastic, 2004.

Harris, Robie H. *I Am NOT Going to School Today*. Simon & Schuster, 2003.

Harrison, Troon. *The Dream Collector*. Kids Can Press, 1999.

Harter, Debbie. *Walking Through the Jungle*. Scholastic, 1997.

Haseley, Dennis. *A Story for Bear*. Harcourt, 2002.

Hathorn, Libby. *Way Home*. Knopf, 2002.

Hatkoff, Isabella. *Owen and Mzee*. Scholastic, 2006.

Hazen, Barbara Shook. *Tight Times*. Viking, 1979.

Heap, Sue. *Red Rockets and Rainbow Jelly*. Penguin, 2003.

Heibreder, Robert. *I Wished for a Unicorn*. Kids Can Press, 2000.

Heide, Florence Parry. *The Day of Ahmed's Secret*. William Morrow, 1990.

— *The Problem with Pulcifer*. HarperCollins, 1982.

— *Sami and the Time of the Troubles*. Clarion, 1992.

— *The Shrinking of Treehorn*. Holiday House, 1971.

— *Some Things Are Scary*. Douglas & McIntyre, 2000.

Heine, Helme. *Friends*. Aladdin, 1997.

Henderson, Kathy. *The Little Boat*. Candlewick, 1995.

Hendry, Frances Mary. *Chandra*. Oxford, 1995.

Henkes, Kevin. *Chester's Way*. HarperCollins, 1998.

— *Chrysanthemum*. HarperCollins, 1991.

— *Julius, Baby of the World*. HarperCollins, 1990.

— *Lily's Purple Plastic Purse*. HarperCollins, 1996.

— *Owen*. HarperCollins, 1993.

— *A Weekend with Wendell*. HarperCollins, 1986.

— *Wemberly Worried*. HarperCollins, 2000.

Hiaasen, Carl. *Hoot*. Knopf, 2002.

Highway, Tomson. *Fox on the Ice*. HarperCollins, 2003.

Hill, Kirkpatrick. *Toughboy and Sister*. Penguin, 1992.

Hirschi, Ron. *Seya's Song*. Sasquatch Books, 1992.

Hoban, Tana. *I Wonder*. Harcourt, 1999.

Hoelwarth, Cathryn Clinton. *The Underbed*. Good Books, 1995.

Hoffman, Mary. *Amazing Grace*. Dutton, 1991.

Honey, Elizabeth. *The Cherry Dress*. Allen & Unwin, 1993.

Hood, Susan. *Bad Hair Day*. Grosset & Dunlap, 1999.

Hooper, Mary. *At the Sign of the Sugared Plum*. Bloomsbury, 2003.

Houghton, Eric. *The Crooked Apple Tree*. Barefoot Books, 1999.

Houston, James. *Tikta'Liktak*. Harcourt Brace, 1965.

Howell, Will C. *I Call It Sky*. Walker & Co, 1999.

Hughes, Shirley. *The Trouble with Jack*. Random House, 1995.

Hume, Stephen Eaton. *Rainbow Bay*. Raincoast, 1997.

Hundal, Nancy. *Camping*. Fitzhenry & Whiteside, 1990.

— *I Heard My Mother Call My Name*. HarperCollins, 1990.

— *November Boots*. HarperCollins, 1993.

— *Prairie Summer*. Fitzhenry & Whiteside, 1990.

Hunter, Jana Novotny. *I Have Feelings*. Scholastic Canada, 2001.

Ibbotson, Eva. *Journey to the River Sea*. Macmillan, 2002.

— *The Star of Kazan*. Macmillan, 2005.

Innocenti, Roberto. *Rose Blanche*. Creative Company, 2001.

Irving, John. *A Sound Like Someone Trying Not to Make a Sound*. Random House, 2004.

Itaya, Satoshi. *Buttons and Bo*. Michael Neugebauer Book, 2004.

James, Simon. *My Friend Whale*. Bantam, 1991.

Jeffers, Oliver. *Lost and Found*. Philomel Books, 2006.

Johnston, Karen. *Mr. Bob's Magic Ride in the Sky*. Whitecap, 2002.

Jones, Rebecca. *Matthew and Tilly*. Puffin, 1995.

Joosse, Barbara M. *I Love You the Purplest*. Chronicle, 1996.

Joyce, William. *A Day with Wilbur Robinson*. Harper Trophy, 1990.

Juster, Norton. *Hello, Good-bye Window*. Hyperion, 2005.

Kadohata, Cynthia. *Weedflowers*. Atheneum, 2006.

Kasza, Keiko. *The Wolf's Chicken Stew*. Putnam, 1987

Katz, Karen. *Counting Kisses*. Simon & Schuster, 2003.

Keats, Ezra Jacks. *The Snowy Day*. Scholastic, 1962.

Kelsey, Elin. *Strange New Species*. Maple Tree Press, 2005.

Khan, Rukhsana. *King of the Skies*. Scholastic Canada, 2001.

Khan, Rukhsana. *The Roses in My Carpet*. Holiday House, 1998.

Kilborne, Sarah S. *Peach and Blue*. Random House Canada, 1994.

Kimmel, Eric. *Pumpkin Head*. Winslow Press, 2001.

King Smith, Dick. *Just Binnie*. Penguin UK, 2004.

Kitamura, Satoshi. *UFO Diary*. Farrar, Straus & Giroux, 1989.

Komaiko, Leah. *Earl's Too Cool For Me*. Harper Trophy, 1988.

Kopelke, Lisa. *The Younger Brother's Survival Guide*. Simon & Schuster, 2006.

Koss, Amy Goldman. *Where Fish Go in Winter*. Putnam, 1987.

Kraft, Robert. *Chocolatina*. BridgeWater Books, 1998.

Kraus, Robert. *Leo the Late Bloomer*. HarperCollins, 1971.

Krensky, Stephen. *My Teacher's Secret Life*. Simon & Schuster, 1996.

Kuskin, Karla. The Upstairs Cat. Clarion/Houghton Mifflin, 2003.

Lahman, Barbara. *Museum Trip*. Houghton Mifflin, 2006.

— *The Red Book*. Houghton Mifflin, 2004.

Laird, Elizabeth. *The Garbage King*. Macmillan, 2003.

Lammie, Karen J. (Ill.). *Oink!* Barrons, 2005.

Lasky, Kathryn. *The Librarian Who Measured the Earth*. Little Brown, 1994.

— *The Night Journey*. Puffin, 1981.

— *Show and Tell Bunnies*. Candlewick, 1998.

Lawrence, Caroline. *Roman Mystery Series*. Orion, 2003.

Lawson, Julie. *Kate's Castle*. Stoddart, 1992.

Leaf, Munro. *Ferdinand*. Puffin, 1936.

Lee, Lyn. *Pog*. Scholastic, 2000.

Lester, Alison. *Imagine*. Houghton Mifflin, 1989.

Lester, Helen. *Hooway for Wodney Wat*. Walter Lorraine, 1989.

— *Me First*. Houghton Mifflin, 1992.

Levine, Ellen. *I Hate English*. Scholastic, 1989.

Levinson, Ricki. *Our Home Is the Sea*. Dutton/Stewart House, 1988.

Lewis, Paul Owen. *Frog Girl*. Whitecap Books, 2001.

— *Grasper: A Young Crab's Discovery*. Whitecap, 1999.

— *The Jupiter Stone*. Beyond Words Publishing, 1995.

— *Storm Boy*. Beyond Words Publishing, 1995.

Lewis, Rob. *Brothers and Sisters*. Hodder, 2003.

Liao, Jimmy. *The Sound of Colors*. Little Brown, 2006.

Lichtenheld, Tom. *What Are You So Grumpy About?* Little Brown, 2003.

Lionni, Leo. *A Color of His Own*. Knopf, 1993.

— *Alexander and the Wind Up Mouse*. Knopf, 1974.

— *Frederick*. Knopf, 1978.

Lishak, Anthony. *Marlene's Magic Birthday*. HarperCollins, 1993.

Little, Jean. *Emma's Yucky Brother* HarperCollins, 2001.

— *Hey World, Here I Am!* HarperCollins, 1986.

— *Willow and Twig*. Puffin, 2000.

Lobel, Arnold. *Fables*. Harper Trophy, 1980.

Loewen, Iris. *My Kokum Called Today*. Pemmican, 2001.

London, Jonathan. *Dream Weaver*. Harcourt Brace, 1998.

— *Into the Night We Are Rising*. Viking, 1993.

— *Like Butter on Pancakes*. Viking, 1995.

— *Liplap's Wish*. Chronicle, 1994.

— *Puddles*. Viking, 1997.

— *The Owl Who Became the Moon*. Dutton/Stewart House, 1993.

Lovell, Patty. *Stand Tall, Molly Lou Melon*. Putnam, 2001.

Loyie, Larry. *As Long As the Rivers Flow*. Vancouver Art Gallery, 2002.

Lucado, Max. *You Are Special*. Crossway Books, 1997.

Ludwig, Trudy. *My Secret Bully*. Tricycle Press, 2005.

McAllister, Angela. *Snow Angel Mini Treasure*. Lothrop, Lee & Shepard, 1993.

McBratney, Sam. *I'm Sorry*. HarperCollins, 2000.

McCaughrean, Geraldine. *My Grandmother's Clock*. HarperCollins, 2002.

McCloskey, Robert. *One Morning in Maine*. Puffin, 1952.

McCoy, Glenn. *The Legend of Spud Murphy*. Hyperion, 2004.

Macdonald, Megan. *Insects Are My Life*. Scholastic, 1995.

McDonnell, Patrick. *The Gift of Nothing*. Little Brown, 2005.

McElligott, Matthew. *Uncle Frank's Pit*. Penguin, 1998.

McFarlane, Sheryl. *Jessie's Island*. Orca, 1992.

McGovern, Ann. *The Lady in the Box*. Turtle Books, 1997.

McGugan, Jim. *Josepha: A Prairie Boy's Story*. Red Deer College Press/Chronicle, 1994.

McLachlan, Patricia. *All the Places to Love*. HarperCollins, 1994.

McNamara, Margaret. *The Playground Problem (Robin Hill School)*. Simon & Schuster, 2004.

McNaughton, Colin. *Once Upon an Ordinary School Day*. Farrar, Straus & Giroux, 2005.

McPhail, David. *Drawing Lessons from a Bear*. Little Brown, 2000.

— *Sisters*. Harcourt Brace, 1984.

— *The Teddy Bear*. Henry Holt, 2002.

Madonna. *Mr. Peabody's Apples*. Calloway, 2003.

Marshall, James. *George and Martha*. Houghton Mifflin, 1972.

— *George and Martha: One Fine Day*. Houghton Mifflin, 1978.

— *George and Martha: Rise and Shine*. Houghton Mifflin, 1976.

Martin Jr., Bill. *Knots on a Counting Rope*. Henry Holt, 1997.

Martin, Rafe. *The Boy Who Lived with the Seals*. Putnam, 1993.

— *The Rough-Face Girl*. Puffin, 2002.

Maynard, Bill. *Incredible Ned*. Putnam. 1997.

Merriam, Eve. *The Wise Woman and Her Secret*. Simon & Schuster, 1991.

Mikaelsen, Ben. *Petey*. Hyperion, 1998.

— *Touching Spirit Bear*. Harper Trophy, 2001.

Miles, Ellen. *Taylor Made Tales: The Dog's Secret*. Scholastic, 2006.

Monnier, Miriam. *Just Right*. North-South Books, 2001.

Monson, A.M. *Wanted: Best Friend*. Scholastic, 1997.

Morpurgo, Michael. *Private Peaceful*. Collins, 2003.

— *Farm Boy*. Pavillion, 1997.

— *War Horse*. Egmont, 1982.

Morrison, Toni. *The Big Box*. Hyperion, 1999.

Moss, Miriam. *Wibble Wobble*. Tiger Tales, 2002.

Munsch, Robert. *The Paper Bag Princess*. Annick, 1980.

Munson, Derek. *Enemy Pie*. Chronicle, 2000.

Murphy, Joanne Brisson. *Feelings*. Black Moss Press, 1985.

Muth, Jon J. *Stone Soup*. Scholastic, 2003.

— *The Three Questions*. Scholastic, 2002.

— *Zen Shorts*. Scholastic, 2005.

Myers, Christopher (Ill). *Wings*. Scholastic, 2000.

Naylor, Phyllis Reynolds. *King of the Playground*. Atheneum, 1991.

Nelson, S.D. *The Star People: A Lakota Story*. Harry N. Abrams, 2003.

Nikly, Michelle. *The Perfume of Memory*. Scholastic Canada, 1999.

Nobisso, Josephine. *Shh! The Whale is Smiling*. Gingerbread House, 1992.

Nolan, Dennis. *Dinosaur Dreams*. Simon & Schuster, 1990.

Nordin, Sofia. *In the Wild*. Groundwood, 2003.

Numeroff, Laura. *What Mommies/Daddies Do Best*. Simon & Schuster, 1998.

Odor, Ruth. *My Quiet Book* . The Child's World, 1977

O'Neill, Alexis. *The Recess Queen*. Scholastic, 2002.

O'Neill, Mary. *Hailstones and Halibut Bones*. Doubleday, 1961.

Oppel, Kenneth. *Silverwing*. HarperCollins, 1998.

Oram, Hiawyn. *What's Naughty?* Hodder, 1984.

— *In the Attic*. Harcourt Brace, 1995.

Ostrow, Jesse. *My Garden*. Scholastic. 1994.

Paolilli, Paul. *Silver Seeds*. Penguin, 2001.

Park, Linda Sue. *A Single Chard*. Dell Yearling, 2001.

Parr, Todd. *It's Okay to Be Different*. Little Brown, 2001.

— *The Peace Book*. Little Brown, 2004.

Patterson, Heather. *A Poppy Is to Remember*. Scholastic Canada, 2004.

Paulson, Gary. *The Hatchet*. (audio book), 1989.

— *The Winter Room*. Thorndike Press, 2005.

Paver, Michelle. *Wolf Brother*. Orion, 2005.

Pearson, Emily. *Ordinary Mary's Extraordinary Deed*. Gibbs Smith, 2002.

Pennypacker, Sara. *Stuart Goes To School*. Scholastic, 2003.

Perry, Sarah. *If*. J. Paul Getty Trust, 1995.

Phillips, Christopher. *The Philosopher's Club*. Tricycle Press, 2001.

Piggot, Dawn. *Gregory and the Magic Line*. Orion, 2002.

Pilkey, Dav. *The Paperboy*. Scholastic, 1996.

Pinkwater, Daniel Manus. *The Big Orange Splot*. Scholastic, 1977.

Plain, Ferguson. *Eagle Feather: An honour*. Pemmican, 2001.

Plourde, Lynn. *Spring's Sprung*. Simon & Schuster, 2002.

— *Summer's Vacation*. Simon & Schuster, 2003.

— *Wild Child*. Simon & Schuster, 2003.

— *Winter Waits*. Simon & Schuster, 2000.

Polacco, Patricia. *Appelemando's Dreams*. Philomel Books, 1991.

— *The Bee Tree*. Philomel Books, 2002.

— *My Rotten Red-Headed Older Brother*. Simon and Schuster, 1994.

Popov. *Why?* North-South Books, 1995.

Raffi. *Baby Beluga*. Crown Books, 1992.

Raschka, Chris. *Ring! Yo?* Orchard Books, 1993.

— *Yo! Yes!* Orchard Books, 1993.

Rathmann, Peggy. *Bootsie Barker Bites*. Puffin, 2002.

— *Ruby the Copycat*. Scholastic, 1991.

Ray, Mary Lyn. *Mud*. Harcourt, 1996.

Reid, Barbara. *The Party*. Scholastic, 1997.

Reynolds, Peter H. *The Dot*. Continuum, 2003.

— *Ish*. Candlewick, 2004.

Robertson, Mark P. *The Egg*. Raincoast, 2000.

— *The Sandcastle*. Raincoast, 2001.

— *Seven Ways to Catch the Moon*. Raincoast, 1999.

Rock, Lois. *I Wonder Why*. Chronicle, 2000.

Rogers, Jacqueline. *Tiptoe into Kindergarten*. Scholastic, 1999.

Rohmann, Eric. *The Cinder-Eyed Cats*. Dragonfly Books, 1997.

— *Clara and Asha*. Roaring Book Press, 2005.

— *Time Flies*. Dragonfly Books, 1994.

Rosen, Michael. *This Is Our House*. Candlewick, 1996.

Rosenberg, Liz. *The Carousel*. San Diego: Voyager Books/Harcourt Brace, 1995.

Rosenberry, Vera. *Vera's First Day of School*. Henry Holt, 1999.

— *When Vera Was Sick*. Henry Holt, 1998.

Rosenthal, Amy Krouse. *Cookies: Bite-Size Life Lessons*. HarperCollins, 2006.

Rowe, Jeannette. *Whose Nose?* Little Brown, 1999.

Ruhmann, Karl. *But I Want To!* NY: North-South Books, 20002.

Russell, Christopher. *Brind and the Dogs of War*. Puffin, 2005.

Ryan, Pam Munoz. *Hello Ocean*. Charlesbridge, 2003

Ryder, Joanne. *Chipmunk Song*. McClelland & Stewart, 1987.

— *Earthdance*. Henry Holt, 1999.

— *Snail's Spell*. NY: Puffin, 1982.

— *The Waterfall's Gift*. Gibbs Smith, 2001.

Rylant, Cynthia. *The Birthday Presents*. Orchard Books, 1987.

— *Every Living Thing*. Atheneum, 1985.

— *In November*. Harcourt, 2000.

— *The Van Gogh Café*. Scholastic, 1995.

— *When I Was Young in the Mountains*. McClelland & Stewart, 1982.

Sachar, Lois. *Holes*. Laurel Leaf, 2001.

— *Small Steps*. Thorndike, 2006.

St. Anthony Catholic School Students. *When I'm Scared*.

St. Pierre, Stephanie. *What the Sea Saw*. Peachtree, 2006.

San Souci, Robert. *Nicholas Pipe*. Dutton, 1997.

Sanderson, Esther. *Two Pairs of Shoes*. Pemmican, 2001.

Say, Allan. *Stranger in the Mirror*. Walter Lorraine, 1995.

Scheer, Julian. *By the Light of the Captured Moon*. Thomas Allen & Son, 2001.

Schuch, Steve. *A Symphony of Whales*. Harcourt, 1999.

Schwartz, Amy. *Annabelle Swift, Kindergartener*. Orchard Books, 1996.

— *Things I Learned in Second Grade*. Orchard Books, 1996.

Sears, Laurie. *Ian's Walk: A story about autism*. Albert Whitman & Co., 2003.

Sendak, Maurice. *Where the Wild Things Are*. HarperCollins, 1963.

Seuss, Dr. *My Many Colored Days*. Knopf, 1996.

Shannon, David. *David Gets in Trouble*. Scholastic Canada, 2002.

— *David Goes to School*. The Bluesky Press, 1999.

— *No, David!* Scholastic, 1998.

Sharmat, Marjorie Weinman. *Big Fat Enormous Lie*. McClelland & Stewart, 1986.

Shearer, Alex. *Tins*. Macmillan, 2006.

Silverstein, Shel. *The Giving Tree*. Harper & Row, 1964.

Simms, Laura. *Rotten Teeth*. Houghton Mifflin, 1998.

Simon, James. *My Friend Whale*. Candlewick, 2003.

Sis, Peter. *Madlenka's Dog*. Farrar, Straus, Giroux, 2002.

Slaughter, Hope. *A Cozy Place*. Red Hen Press, 1999.

Smith, Alexander McCall. *Akimbo and the Lions*. Egmont, 2005.

Snyder, Zilpha Keatly. *The Changeling*. Simon & Schuster, 1970.

Snihura, Ulana. *I Miss Franklin B. Shuckles*. Annick, 1998.

Spalding, Andrea. *Me and Mr. Mah*. Orca, 1999.

— *Solomon's Tree*. Orca, 2002.

Spinelli, Eileen. *Sophie's Masterpiece*. Simon & Schuster, 2001.

Spinelli, Jerry. *Fourth Grade Rats*. Scholastic, 1991.

— *Loser*. Harper Trophy, 2002.

— *Star Girl*. Laurel Leaf, 2000.

— *Wringer*. Harper Trophy, 1997.

Steig, William. *Amos and Boris*. Farrar, Straus & Giroux, 1971.

— *Brave Irene*. Farrar, Straus & Giroux, 1986.

— *Dr. DeSoto*. Farrar, Straus & Giroux, 1982.

— *Spinky Sulks*. Farrar, Straus & Giroux, 1988.

— *Sylvester and the Magic Pebble*. Simon & Schuster, 1969.

Stinson, Kathy. *Big or Little*. Annick, 1983.

— *Mom and Dad Don't Live Together Anymore*. Annick, 1999.

— *Red is Best*. Annick, 1982.

Stroud, Jonathan. *Buried Fire*. Hyperion, 1999.

Swope, Sam. *The Araboolies of Liberty Street*. Crown, 1989.

Tan, Shaun. *The Red Tree*. Simply Read Books, 2004.

Tavares, Matt. *Zachary's Ball*. Candlewick, 2000.

Taylor, C.J. *The Secret of the White Buffalo*. Tundra, 1997.

Taylor, Cora. *Ghost Voyage (I, II, III)*. Coteau, 2004.

Taylor, Theodore. *Ice Drift*. Harcourt, 2005.

Teague, Mark. *Lost and Found.*: Scholastic, 1998.

— *The Secret Short Cut*. Scholastic, 1996.

Thomas, Frances. *The Bear and Mr. Bear*. Dutton, 1995.

Thomas, Shelley Moore. *Somewhere Today: A Book of Peace*. Albert Whitman & Co, 1998.

Thompson, Richard. *Then and Now*. Fitzhenry & Whiteside, 1999.

Thomson, Sarah. *Imagine a Day*. Atheneum, 2005.

— *Imagine a Night*. Atheneum, 2003.

Thong, Roseanne. *Round Is a Mooncake*. Scholastic, 2000.

Tibo, Gilles. *Shy Guy*. North-South Books, 2002.

Tomlinson, Jill. *The Owl Who Was Afraid of the Dark*. Egmont, 2004.

Tresslet, Alvin. *Rain, Drop, Splash*. HarperCollins, 1990.

— *White Snow, Bright Snow*. HarperCollins, 1947.

Trottier, Maxine. *Claire's Gift*. Scholastic, 1999.

— *Dreamstones*. Stoddart, 1999.

— *Flags*. Stoddart, 1999.

— *The Tiny Kite of Eddie Wing*. Stoddart, 1995.

Tsuchiya, Yukio. *Faithful Elephants: A True Story of Animals, People and War*. Houghton Mifflin, 1988.

Turkle, Brinton. *Do Not Open*. Dutton/Stewart House, 1981.

Udry, Janice May. *A Tree Is Nice*. HarperCollins, 1956.

Vaage, Carol. *Bibi and the Bull*. Red Deer College Press, 1996.

Van Allsburg, Chris. *The Garden of Abdul Gasazi*. Houghton Mifflin, 1979.

— *Jumanji*. Scholastic, 1985.

— *Just a Dream*. Houghton Mifflin, 1990.

— *The Mysteries of Harris Burdick*. Houghton Mifflin, 1984.

— *The Polar Express*. Houghton Mifflin, 1985.

— *The Stranger*. Houghton Mifflin, 1986.

— *The Sweetest Fig*. Houghton Mifflin, 1993.

— *The Widow's Broom*. Houghton Mifflin, 1992.

— *The Wretched Stone*. Houghton Mifflin, 1991.

— *Zathura*. Houghton Mifflin, 2002.

Van Draanen, Wendelin. *Flipped*. Knopf, 2001.

— *The Shredderman Series*. Yearling, 2006.

Van Laan, Nancy. *Little Fish Lost*. Aladdin, 1998.

— *Rainbow Crow*. Random House, 1989.

Vaughan, Richard Lee. *Eagle Boy: Pacific Northwest Native Tale*. Sasquatch, 2000.

Viorst, Judith. *Alexander and the Terrible, Horrible, No Good, Very Bad Day*. Atheneum, 1971.

— *Earrings*. Aladdin, 1990.

— *The Good-bye Book*. Aladdin, 1992.

— *If I Were in Charge of the World and Other Worries*. Atheneum, 1981.

— *Rosie and Michael*. Aladdin, 1974.

— *Super Completely and Totally the Messiest*. Atheneum, 2001.

— *The Tenth Good Thing about Barney*. Atheneum, 1974.

Waber, Bernard. *Courage*. Houghton Mifflin, 2002.

— *Ira Sleeps Over*. Houghton Mifflin, 1972.

Waboose, Jan Bourdeau. *Morning on the Lake*. Kids Can Press, 1998.

— *Sky Sisters*. Kids Can Press, 2000.

Waddell, Martin. *Farmer Duck*. Candlewick, 1991.

Walker, Alice. *Finding the Green Stone*. Harcourt Brace, 1997.

Wallace, Ian. *Boy of the Deeps*. Douglas & McIntyre, 1999.

— *Chin Chang and the Dragon Dance*. Simon & Schuster, 1984.

Wallace, John. *Tiny Rabbit Goes to a Birthday Party*. Puffin, 2000.

Walsh, Melanie. *My World, Your World*. Doubleday, 2004.

Wargin, Kathy-Jo. *The Legend of the Loon*. Gale Group, 2000.

Watt, Melanie. *Scaredy Squirrel*. Kids Can, 2006

Weiss, George David. *What a Wonderful World*. Atheneum, 1995.

Wells, Rosemary. *Night Sounds, Morning Colors*. Dutton, 1996.

— *Shy Charles*. Puffin, 1988.

— *Timothy Goes to School*. Puffin, 1981.

Whetung, James. *The Vision Seeker*. Stoddart, 1997.

White Deer of Autumn. *The Great Change*. Beyond Words Publishing, 1993.

Wiesner, David. *Free Fall*. Lothrop, Lee & Shepard/William Morrow, 1988.

— *Hurricane*. Clarion, 1990.

— *June 29, 1999*. Clarion, 1992.

— *The Three Pigs*. Clarion, 2001.

— *Tuesday*. Clarion, 1991.

Wild, Margaret. *Fox*. Kane-Miller, 2000.

Wilhelm, Hans. *I'll Always Love You*. Dragonfly Books, 1985.

Willems, Mo. *Knuffle Bunny*. Scholastic, 2004.

Williams, Maiya. *The Golden Hour*. Amulet, 2006

Williams, Vera B. *A Chair for My Mother*. HarperCollins, 1984.

Willis, Jeanne. *Dumb Creatures*. Macmillan, 2004.

Wilson, Troy. *The Perfect Man*. Orca, 2004.

Winter, Jeanette. *Mama*. Harcourt, 2006.

Withers, Pam. *Raging River*. Walrus Books, 2003.

Wood, Audrey. *The Flying Dragon Room*. Scholastic, 2000.

— *Quick as a Cricket*. Child's Play International, 1989.

Wood, Douglas. *A Quiet Place*. Simon & Schuster, 2002.

Worth, Valerie. *All the Small Poems, Plus Fourteen More*. Farrar, Straus & Giroux, 1987.

Wynne-Jones, Tim. *Architect of the Moon*. Douglas & McIntyre, 1988.

—*The Maestro*. Douglas & McIntyre, 1995.

Yee, Paul. *The Bone Collector's Son*. Tradewind, 2003.

Yolen, Jane. *Owl Moon*. Philomel, 2002.

— *Before the Storm*. Boyds Mills, 1995.

Young, Ed. *Seven Blind Mice*. Putnam, 2002.

Zimmermann, Werner. *Snow Day*. Scholastic Canada, 1999.

Zolotow, Charlotte. *The Seashore Book*. HarperCollins, 1992.

— *The Unfriendly Book*. Harper & Row, 1975.

— *When the Wind Stops*. HarperTrophy, 1995.

— *William's Doll*. HarperCollins, 1972.

Zonta, Pat. *Jessica's X-Ray*. Firefly, 2001.

Index